HOW TO FIND YOUR TECHY SOULMATE

A COMPREHENSIVE DATING GUIDE FOR INTROVERTS AND NERDS IN INDIA

RO_____N PATEL

Contents

PROLOGUE

I will admit, I love Star Wars and Star Trek. A big fan of most Marvel movies too. Spidey, The Avengers, and other superhero movies have become a means of unwinding in my private time.

Born in the seventies, I have seen most science fiction movies and series out there. Next to sci-fi and other genres, 'The Big Bang Theory', a comedy series in which three brilliant scientists struggle to find love, is one of my all-time favorites and a great source of recognition.

In my professional life, I love my work as an IT entrepreneur. I also have a passion for high tech. When I am not working for my clients, I always have a side project or two to keep me busy. By this time, you might have guessed, this guy must be a classic nerd. And... you are correct. I prefer to be addressed as an introverted and tech-savvy individual.

In my youth, I tried hard to belong to a certain group of friends, trying to fit that extrovert ideal, until one night, I came home, exhausted from a night out socializing with some friends. Suddenly, I realized that the overstimulation of many people in a room with loud music depleted my energy levels. I was in my twenties, a student who was discovering his place in this world.

During my years at university, I learned that I enjoyed being with friends and attending social events, but I enjoyed my time alone even more. During that period in my life, I experienced social pressure from classmates to join them at parties, to the point where it exhausted me. Not much later, I decided to only go to events that really interested me and skip the rest.

Over the years, I learned there are different degrees of introversion. No one is completely an introvert or completely an extrovert. On a scale from 1 to 100, I guess I am an introvert for 70% and 30% an extrovert. Although this 30% enables me to speak in front of groups, these events really drain my energy. At the end of such days, I longed for a good laugh watching an episode with Sheldon, Leonard, and Raj.

Fast-forwarding to 2024, I started the second half of my life as a happy father of two beautiful kids and a partner I have loved since the day I met her.

So, how did I do this as an introvert and 'nerd' who is passionate about his work? I am not a relationship therapist, nor do I have a psychology background. My academic titles in business education will not help either. I am simply an expert by experience.

My roots in India and upbringing in Western Europe enable me to connect two worlds: East and West, and appreciate both sides.

I wrote this book to help my fellow introverts, nerds, and geeks find their soulmates. I will walk with you through the path where you no longer try to be an extrovert but start embracing your introversion and grow to a state where you are ready for multiple adventures on your journey for love.

During my research for this book, I used my skills as a nerd and learned many things about relationship therapy, psychology, and digital marketing. I learned a lot about myself but also about my fellow introverts. I translated this into many practical tips and guidelines for my readers to travel safely in the online dating multiverse.

My love for India has made me decide to start helping introverts in the country of my ancestors. As an Overseas Citizen of India, I decided to give something back to a culture rich in tradition but also struggling to find love in the era of online dating. Therefore, when I write 'in India', you can read 'introverts with Indian roots'.

This book is the first part of a series. By the time of publishing, I hope to have finished the US and EU editions since each region and country has its own customs and traditions.

I hope you enjoy reading my first published book, and in case you have any questions or feedback on how to make the content better to serve our fellow introverts, feel free to leave a comment on my website techysoulmates.com.

I

The Changing Landscape of Love in India

The Evolution of Romance

Let's start with a simple truth: love in India has always been a bit of an adventure. But in the past few decades, that adventure has shifted gears dramatically. It is like moving from black-and-white TV straight into the world of virtual reality, where dating apps, online profiles, and instant connections are now part of the landscape. For an introvert, nerd, or someone who does not quite fit the mold, this new world of romance can feel both exciting and, let's be honest, a little intimidating.

If you rewind a couple of generations, love and marriage in India were not really about individual choices. Families played the biggest role, with parents and elders making the important decisions. You would be 'introduced' to a potential match, usually in a family setting. And while there might be some nervous glances and quick exchanges, the real discussions about marriage happened between families rather than the people actually getting married. Love was often something that grew over time, if it grew at all. It was built on the foundation of duty, compatibility, and tradition, not necessarily personal connection or attraction.

Back then, romance was not about swiping right or scrolling through profiles but about commitment—plain and simple. The idea of meeting someone for a coffee to 'see if there's a spark' would have been nearly unthinkable. You did not date. You got married and then discovered who you were married to, gradually unfolding layers as life progressed.

But then, as the world started shrinking with the internet, television, and exposure to Western media, things began to change. People saw different kinds of relationships portrayed on screen—friendship-based, passion-driven, and even soul-deep connections that felt far more personal than traditional arranged marriages. Bollywood, too, started to reflect this shift, with films that moved beyond just singing around trees and dived into real stories of love and heartbreak. Suddenly, the idea of 'choosing' your partner gained ground.

This shift meant that people started wanting more from their relationships. Instead of settling into a predefined role, young Indians began dreaming of love stories that resonated with their personalities. For introverts, geeks, and people with niche interests, this was both a blessing and a new challenge. You could, in theory, find someone who shared your love for astrophysics or your obsession with Marvel movies, but where would you start looking? The traditional methods did not account for personal passion or interest compatibility.

In the 2000s, India saw the entry of dating websites. At first, these were considered a bit taboo or something for the 'modern' crowd, often dismissed by the more conservative groups as being unsuitable for serious relationships. But as the years rolled on, online dating began to break into the mainstream, creating a new space for young Indians to explore. No longer limited to arranged introductions, people could now connect based on shared interests, similar backgrounds, or even just mutual attraction.

And then came the dating apps, the ultimate game-changer. Suddenly, you did not just have a few profiles on a website to browse. Instead, you had a near-endless stream of potential matches right at your fingertips. Tinder, Bumble, TrulyMadly, and Hinge burst onto the scene, each offering their own spin on how you could meet people. For someone like me—who grew up knowing only one version of how love and marriage work—it is fascinating to see how completely different the dating landscape looks now.

Of course, these changes brought along new complexities, especially for those of us who do not fit the outgoing, social ideal. The introverts, the nerds, the geeks—we have had to adapt to a dating culture that can sometimes feel more like a popularity contest than a genuine search for a connection. Unlike traditional introductions, where family acts as a sort of buffer, dating apps place us directly in the spotlight, where the pressure is on to make a quick, appealing impression.

For many introverts, this has been an uncomfortable shift. Attempts at small talk, endless profile swiping, and the fear of being 'ghosted' (yes, it is as unsettling as it sounds) can be overwhelming. Dating apps are built around the idea of instant attraction, and for people who crave depth and value meaningful connections, this can feel unnatural. But, on the flip side, it is also liberating to be in control of your own choices and to seek out people who genuinely resonate with you.

In today's India, love has evolved into a mix of tradition and modernity. While the influence of family is still present, the balance has tipped towards individual choice. People can now openly date, explore, and take their time getting to know each other before making big commitments. Yet, the weight of cultural expectations lingers in the background, especially when it comes to marriage. Even if you meet someone on an app and connect with them on a deeply personal level, there's often the question of whether your family will accept the relationship, or if your backgrounds align enough to 'make it work.'

For someone with roots in both India and the West, I find this blend of old and new fascinating. There's a respect for tradition, yet a desire for personal happiness and compatibility. This shift reflects a new India, where people are redefining romance in ways that reflect their personalities, interests, and values. You could say that, just like India itself, love here is in a state of transformation, continuously evolving and finding its own unique balance.

So, where does this leave us—the introverts, nerds, and geeks? It means we are now in a world where finding love is more accessible than ever, but also more complex. We have options, but we also have to be clearer about who we are and what we are looking for. And in a culture where the idea of 'self-love' is still relatively new, this journey can be as much about understanding ourselves as it is about finding someone else.

As we explore this new terrain together, remember that there's no one-size-fits-all approach to finding love. Whether through traditional methods, online dating, or even a random encounter at a bookstore (one can dream, right?), the essence of connection remains the same. It is about finding someone who appreciates you for exactly who you are—whether that is a Star Wars-loving, Marvel-watching, introverted techie, or someone entirely different.

The journey of love in modern India is a mix of discovery, patience, and embracing both old and new. As we discover this path, it is worth remembering that love is, at its heart, an adventure—one that is as much about finding the right person as it is about understanding what truly makes us happy.

The Role of Online Dating in India

There was a time when dating in India was hardly 'dating' as we know it today. The idea of finding love by yourself, outside of arranged marriages, was something people read about in novels or saw in Bollywood movies. Fast forward a few decades and online dating has made its way into India, completely transforming how people approach relationships.

When I first heard about dating apps making waves in India, I was curious and a little skeptical. Let's be honest—this is a country where family, community, and tradition shape nearly every aspect of life, especially relationships. The concept of meeting someone online, a total stranger, and choosing them without family involvement was almost unthinkable just a few years ago. But online dating came along and quietly changed the rules.

The shift started slowly. Initially, online dating was considered 'Western', a concept that did not quite fit into India's family-oriented culture. People viewed it with suspicion, thinking it was only for those who were not 'serious' about relationships or did not care about tradition. But as more Indians got access to the internet, dating apps found their way into the hands of a young generation that was ready for something different. For these young people, online dating became a way to explore and connect on their terms. It offered freedom—freedom to choose, to chat, to meet, and yes, even to decide when to move forward.

For introverts, geeks, and those of us who do not quite fit into traditional social settings, online dating has been a blessing. It means we do not have to rely on the old ways, where families get involved from the start, making introductions in front of everyone and piling on the pressure. Instead, online dating lets us meet people without that immediate layer of family scrutiny. You can take your time, chat from the comfort of your own space, and figure out if there's a connection before even thinking about any introductions.

India's dating app scene has grown exponentially, and with that, the variety of platforms available has expanded too. Each app has its own vibe and its own unwritten rules. Tinder became a hit because it is quick, simple, and popular among people in big cities who are used to swiping through choices. Bumble, on the other hand, has attracted people who like the idea of women making the first move, which is still a big cultural shift here. TrulyMadly focuses more on compatibility, making it appealing to those who are looking for more than a casual fling. With all these options, people can choose an app that suits their personality and preferences.

One of the things I find fascinating about online dating in India is how it balances modern individuality with cultural roots. Dating apps here are not just about instant attraction; they are often used by people who are genuinely looking for someone who 'fits' their lives. Many users still have traditional expectations around marriage and family, even if they are open to dating outside of their community or city. It is a sort of hybrid model—a blend of old and new, where people seek personal compatibility but still keep family values and future marriage in mind. It is dating with one foot in modernity and the other in tradition.

The beauty of online dating, especially for introverts, is that it puts us in control. You get to decide when you are ready to take a conversation from the digital world into the real one. No need for small talk in noisy cafés or bars if that is not your scene. You can build rapport, let conversations evolve naturally, and even spend a few days just messaging before deciding to meet. For someone who likes a slower pace or prefers meaningful conversations, this control makes the process a lot more comfortable.

But there's another side to it, too. While online dating has brought new possibilities, it also has its own challenges. The 'swipe culture' that apps promote can feel shallow or even exhausting. When you are just one of the countless profiles that people swipe through, it is easy to feel lost or like you have to put on a 'digital persona' to stand out. For people who value depth and authenticity, this can be tricky. How do you show the real 'you' in a few photos and a short bio?

And then, of course, there's ghosting—something almost everyone on a dating app experiences at some point. Unlike traditional settings where families stay connected and act as intermediaries, online dating gives people the option to disappear without a word. For those of us who invest time and emotion into our conversations, this can be discouraging. Introverts and people who open up slowly can feel especially vulnerable here, as the idea of someone vanishing mid-conversation feels like an abrupt end that is hard to move past.

Despite these challenges, online dating has undeniably given people a way to break out of old patterns. It has allowed young Indians to redefine what dating means in a way that fits their personalities, interests, and, yes, even quirks. For nerds and geeks who have a hard time finding someone who shares their love for sci-fi, tech, or other niche interests, dating apps have opened up an entirely new pool of people who might just 'get' them.

In a way, online dating in India is like testing new waters with familiar landmarks on the horizon. People can explore romance independently but still keep an eye on the cultural expectations they grew up with. For some, this means building connections without family involvement until they are serious. For others, it is a way to meet people outside their immediate social circles, people they would not have encountered in traditional matchmaking settings.

As online dating continues to grow in India, the balance between individuality and tradition will likely keep shifting. More young people are seeing dating as a journey rather than a race to marriage, and they are using these platforms to find not just a partner but a companion who understands them. And for those of us who thrive in one-on-one settings, dating apps offer a way to skip the noise and go straight to what matters—connecting on a personal level.

It is clear that online dating in India is not just a trend; it is becoming a new norm, especially for urban professionals and young adults who crave choice and agency. For introverts, nerds, and everyone else who may have felt out of place in traditional setups, this evolution means there's finally space to explore relationships on our terms. Whether it leads to lasting love, a short-lived romance, or just a few memorable conversations, online dating has carved out a place in the Indian dating landscape, offering options that simply did not exist before.

In the end, the role of online dating in India is still unfolding. But it has already shown us one important thing: love and connection can adapt, even in a country rich in tradition. And for all of us on this journey, whether we are meeting people online or offline, the opportunity to create our path in love is a powerful shift—a way of merging who we are with who we hope to find.

Introducing Our Audience – Introverts, Nerds, Geeks, and the Tech-Savvy

When I think about who this book is really for, it is easy to picture the faces of fellow introverts, nerds, geeks, and tech-savvy folks who have found themselves engaging in the world of dating while feeling a bit out of place. Let's be honest—dating as an introvert, or as someone who is more into coding than clubbing, is not always straightforward. And in a culture like India's, where there are strong expectations about how relationships should form, it can feel like an even bigger challenge.

This book is for those of us who grew up feeling like we did not quite fit into traditional social molds. Maybe you are someone who prefers a good book over a bustling party or finds more excitement in a late-night gaming session than in small talk with strangers. Or perhaps you are a curious mind, fascinated by science, technology, or stories that explore far-off galaxies. If you have ever wondered whether there's someone out there who will 'get' you, quirks and all, this journey is meant to help you find that connection.

The idea of putting ourselves out there, making small talk, and keeping up with the pace of traditional dating can feel exhausting. I get it—it is a world that seems set up for extroverts, with meet-ups and dates often happening in loud, crowded spaces where quick impressions seem to matter more than real conversations. But here is the good news: dating does not have to be a test of extroversion. There's a way to approach it that aligns with who we are, respects our need for depth, and values connection over endless chatter.

And for the geeks and nerds among us—the ones who can talk about the intricacies of Star Wars timelines or debate the best Marvel movie—dating can sometimes feel like a constant 'hide-and-reveal' game. How much of your passion do you show upfront? Will they appreciate your love for tech or think it is 'too much'? This book is for those of you who have faced that internal debate about sharing your interests and wonder if there's someone out there who will not only accept them but maybe even share them. Spoiler alert: there are people who will appreciate you exactly as you are, but sometimes it takes a little guidance to find them.

This book is also written for people who may have tried the traditional ways of meeting someone, only to feel like they are forcing themselves to fit a mold that does not feel natural. Indian culture, as rich and vibrant as it is, often carries expectations about relationships that can make dating a bit challenging for people who walk their own path.

Later in this book, you will find that Indian culture does not mean 'only in India'. As a child with ancestors from India, tradition and customs were exported to other countries like Suriname (Latin America), the UK, and the Netherlands (Europe). In these traditions and customs, there is still a lot of pressure to find a partner in a way that aligns with family expectations and community norms. For those who do not naturally follow those norms, it is easy to feel like you are somehow falling behind or missing out. But love is not one-size-fits-all, and it is absolutely possible to find a partner who respects your individuality.

Whether you are someone who is just starting to explore the world of online dating or someone who is already had a few ups and downs along the way, this book aims to be a practical companion on your journey. I have filled it with real world advice, thoughtful insights, and strategies that align with your personality, your pace, and your passions. It is designed to help you navigate this path without sacrificing who you are or pretending to be someone you are not. If you have been looking for a way to date authentically without the pressure to act like an extrovert or to downplay what makes you unique, you are in the right place.

I also want to acknowledge the unique mix of tradition and modernity that shapes dating in India today. For many of us, this means figuring out how to balance our own preferences with family expectations, something that is not always easy. There's the feeling of wanting to be true to yourself but also respecting the values you were raised with. And while dating apps have opened up new ways to meet people, they come with their own set of challenges, especially for those of us who crave connection rather than just endless swiping. This book recognizes those challenges and offers ways to meet them with confidence.

In short, this book is for everyone who feels like they are experiencing the dating world a little differently. It is for the quiet souls who do not crave the spotlight, for the thinkers who would rather connect over meaningful conversations than casual banter, and for the enthusiasts who want someone who appreciates their passions as much as they do. You will find practical tips, encouragement, and some hard-earned wisdom here—all aimed at helping you find a partner who values you for exactly who you are.

If you have ever felt like the dating world was not designed with you in mind, know that you are not alone. There are others out there, just like you, hoping to find someone who values the qualities that make them unique. So, let's start on this journey together, with the confidence that finding love does not have to mean changing who we are. This book is not about 'fixing' you to fit into dating culture—it is about helping you find a path that aligns with your strengths, your personality, and your dreams for a meaningful relationship.

Whether you are an introvert who treasures quiet moments, a nerd who finds joy in niche interests, or someone who is simply looking for a way to connect authentically, this book is your guide. Here is to embracing what makes us different, and to discovering that true connection is possible, even in a world that often tells us we should be something else.

II
Understanding Cultural Expectations and Barriers

Family and Societal Expectations

If there's one thing you can count on when it comes to dating in India, it is that family and society will always have a say—whether you want them to or not. In most Indian families, relationships are rarely just between two people. There's an entire network of expectations, traditions, and opinions that come along with every match. And while this might make finding a partner feel like maneuvering through a maze, it is also part of what makes Indian culture unique.

Growing up, most of us were taught to value family approval. It is not just about being in a relationship; it is about finding someone who can 'fit' with our family, someone who can easily integrate into our lives and our traditions. This expectation often comes from a place of love—parents and elders want to see their children happy, secure, and in a lasting partnership. But for introverts and people who walk a slightly different path, this can add an extra layer of pressure.

For people like us, who may not always feel comfortable in the traditional social scene, this family-centered approach to relationships can feel a bit like performing for an audience. Imagine going on a first date not just with one person, but with the invisible presence of every relative who has an opinion on who would be 'right' for you. And let's be real, they do have opinions. Aunties and uncles, neighbors, even family friends—they are all invested in the outcome. It is like dating with a live studio audience, waiting to weigh in on every move.

In many Indian families, relationships are seen as a family affair. A potential partner is not just your choice; they are expected to be a choice the whole family can accept. And often, that 'acceptance' comes with a long list of criteria. The person should be from a similar background, belong to the same (or an acceptable) religion or caste, and have a compatible family structure. For introverts or people with a more personal, independent approach, this level of scrutiny can feel overwhelming. How do you find someone who makes you happy while ticking off a family-approved checklist?

This kind of family involvement can make it hard to explore and experiment. Even the idea of 'dating' can raise eyebrows. There's often this unspoken rule that if you are seeing someone, it must be serious—something that will lead to marriage. So, if you are just trying to get to know someone without rushing into a commitment, it can feel like you are bending the rules or stepping out of line. For introverts, who may need more time to open up and feel comfortable, this pressure to 'declare' intentions early can add stress to an already delicate situation.

Then there's society at large. Beyond the family, there's the community—the wider circle of people who, even if they are not directly involved, still seem to have a say in how things should be done. Society brings its own set of norms and expectations, often reinforcing traditional views on relationships. This is where things can get complicated for those of us who do not quite fit into the 'traditional' box. When society expects you to follow a set path, any deviation can feel like an act of rebellion.

Take, for example, the idea of public displays of affection. Even something as simple as holding hands can feel like a bold move in a country where love is still expected to be private, reserved, and sometimes hidden from view. For many of us who value one-on-one connection over public display, this expectation can be a relief. But it also adds another layer engaging into relationships—knowing that society may be watching, judging, and occasionally gossiping.

And then there's the big one: marriage. In Indian culture, marriage is not just a partnership between two people; it is seen as a merging of two families. So, when you are dating, especially online, there's this underlying question: Is this person someone who could become part of my family, too? For introverts, geeks, and people who take relationships seriously, this expectation can feel like a double-edged sword. On one hand, it is a reminder of the importance of commitment and stability. On the other hand, it can create a feeling that you are being evaluated not just for love but for your ability to 'fit' into a role that may not align with who you are.

Meeting these cultural expectations is not easy, but understanding them can make the journey smoother. Family and societal expectations are deeply rooted in values that are central to Indian culture: respect, honor, and a sense of belonging. They come from a place of love and tradition. But at the same time, they can sometimes make it hard for individuals to find the space to discover what they truly want in a partner.

So, what is the way forward? For those of us who do not naturally fit the mold, it is about finding a balance. It is about respecting the importance of family while also carving out room for personal happiness. You do not have to reject family and societal expectations entirely, but you also do not have to mold yourself to meet them perfectly. Instead, focus on finding someone who appreciates you for who you are and understands that while family is important, personal compatibility matters just as much.

This book is here to support you as you navigate these waters. The goal is not to change the way Indian culture views relationships overnight. Instead, it is about finding ways to respect cultural expectations without sacrificing your sense of self. Love can flourish within tradition, but it can also make space for the individual. It is a balance—one that each of us has to find in our own way.

If you are an introvert or someone with unique interests and passions, remember that there's room for you in this landscape. You do not have to compromise who you are to meet family or societal expectations. By being clear about what you value and the kind of connection you are looking for, you can find a path that honors both tradition and individuality.

In the end, family and society may play a role in shaping our relationships, but they do not define them. The heart of any relationship lies between two people who respect, understand, and genuinely connect with each other. So, as you explore the world of dating, remember that while the voices of family and society are there, your own voice matters, too. Embrace it, stay true to yourself, and let that be your guide.

Traditional vs. Modern Mindsets

In the previous section, I explained the role of families in relationships in Indian culture and society. It almost looks like a push and pull between tradition and modernity. On one side, we have centuries-old customs that shape ideas of love and marriage, passed down through generations. On the other, there's a growing mindset centered around personal choice, compatibility, and even love at first sight. For anyone looking for a relationship here, especially if you are someone who does not quite fit the mold, this contrast can feel both freeing and complicated.

Let's start with the traditional perspective. In many Indian families, marriage is more than just a relationship between two people. It is viewed as the coming together of families, cultures, and sometimes even entire communities. Love, in this view, is not necessarily the starting point. Instead, it is seen as something that can grow with time, nurtured within a stable, family-approved partnership. Marriage is valued for its stability, its shared responsibilities, and its role in upholding family values.

Tradition brings with it a sense of security and structure. There's a belief that when a relationship is built on shared values and family support, it will be solid and lasting. For those who feel comforted by these familiar structures, traditional marriages can be deeply fulfilling. But for those of us who are introverts, nerds, geeks, or people with a less conventional outlook, this model can feel restrictive. It does not always make room for individuality or a slower, quieter pace we might need to get close to someone.

Traditional setups often come with a long checklist: family background, education, and social status. And if you are looking for a partner who understands your quirks, shares your interests, or values your independence, fitting into these predefined expectations can feel challenging. It can feel like you are expected to set aside your own personality to 'fit' an ideal that does not match who you truly are.

Then we have the modern approach, which has been steadily growing, especially in cities, over the past few decades. This perspective places a high value on individual choice. Here, relationships are about two people finding common ground based on mutual interests, personality, and emotional connection—without the immediate involvement of extended family. Love and compatibility are often seen as the foundation for commitment, not just a nice addition.

The modern approach allows for a freedom that did not exist in previous generations. People are looking for partners who connect with them on a personal level. They are after relationships that bring friendship, understanding, and emotional support. Individual choice and personal freedom are given priority, so there's room for two people to create a partnership that feels right for them, not just for their families. This shift reflects a new kind of independence—one that celebrates finding someone who complements you as an individual rather than as part of a family unit.

But, as freeing as this can be, it comes with its own set of challenges. For introverts and those who value genuine, slower-paced connections, the fast, often superficial nature of online dating and 'swipe culture' can feel like a poor match. The focus on instant attraction and quick judgments can be overwhelming, especially if what you are seeking is someone who values depth and meaningful connection. While independence is liberating, it can also feel a bit lonely in a world that prioritizes casual connections over building something lasting.

The differences between traditional and modern mindsets can leave many of us feeling caught in between.

Maybe you appreciate the sense of support that comes with family involvement but also want the freedom to choose someone based on compatibility. Or perhaps you value the idea of a committed partnership but are not entirely comfortable with the checklist that traditional marriages often come with. It is not about picking one side or the other but finding a balance that feels true to who you are.

Both mindsets come with their strengths and challenges. Traditional values bring structure, family support, and a focus on long-term stability. Meanwhile, the modern approach emphasizes independence, personal connection, and the freedom to choose a partner based on shared interests and attraction. Many people today find that they want a little of both—a balance that allows for individuality while still valuing family bonds.

For those of us who do not fit neatly into one category, it is worth considering what aspects of each approach feel right to us. What do you want in a relationship? Do you lean towards the sense of belonging that comes with tradition, or the self-expression that modern relationships offer? And do not hesitate to communicate this to potential partners. Understanding each other's values early on can help you find a connection that respects both of your perspectives.

It is also important to remember that blending traditional and modern mindsets does not have to mean compromising who you are. You do not have to give up your individuality to find stability, nor do you have to let go of family values to create a modern relationship. Many couples today are finding ways to honor both approaches, creating partnerships where each person's freedom and family values can coexist. For instance, you might choose to introduce your partner to your family only when you are both ready, allowing your relationship to develop naturally before involving others.

The goal is not to fit yourself into one box or the other but to find someone who respects both sides of you. Someone who values your independence but also appreciates the importance of family ties. Someone who understands that you want the space to grow as a person but also believes in the stability that comes from shared values. It is about building a relationship that respects who you are—a blend that feels both grounded and true to yourself.

In the end, whether you lean more towards traditional values, modern ideas, or somewhere in between, what matters most is finding someone who appreciates your unique perspective. Relationships are no longer a one-size-fits-all experience, and that is something worth celebrating. There's room for both tradition and individual choice in today's world. So, as you explore dating, remember that you are free to create your own path—one that honors both your roots and your individuality.

Impact on Introverts and Non-Conformists

Dating in India, for introverts and non-conformists, often feels like Rajesh Koothrappali trying to talk to a woman without a drink in his hand—awkward, nervewracking, and full of pressure to perform. There's always this loud, unrelenting background noise of societal norms, family values, and unsolicited advice from every corner. If you are someone who prefers quiet connections or refuses to follow the typical social script, it can feel like you are dancing to the wrong song, in the wrong room, with the wrong crowd.

My first experiences with dating went pretty much the same as with Rajesh. Without a beer in my hand, I lacked the courage to speak to girls. My first kiss was only possible after having a couple of beers and some social pressure from my friends in a bar. I think I was around the age of 19 for my first kissing experience. As a child from parents whose grandparents have lived in India, I clearly remember that day I told my father I had a girlfriend; he wanted to see her. She was a native Dutch, with green eyes and blond hair, not with Indian roots, which my parents preferred in the first place. Not because they were concerned about the different cultures between Hindustani and Dutch, but more if I was going to have proper Indian food in this relationship. After some time, my parents found I was serious about her; they started making long-term plans just in case.

I think you now understand that, as an introvert, dating was a bit of a marathon I did not sign up for. Add in the pressure to 'perform' for my family and societal approval, and it starts feeling like Raj at a party, standing in a corner, smiling nervously while wishing he was somewhere else entirely. Just like with my own experiences, traditional Indian dating often prioritizes quick introductions, family involvement, and ticking off compatibility checklists. For introverts who like to take their time, build trust slowly, and savor deep conversations, this setup can feel like a sprint when all you want is a thoughtful stroll.

And let's not forget the non-conformists—the people who march to their own rhythm, whether that is through an obsession with astronomy, a passion for cosplay, or a love for fantasy novels. Dating in India is like Raj trying to explain his love for poetry and planetary movements at a family dinner—met with polite nods at best, or confusion and dismissal at worst. The same goes for introverts with Indian roots, like me. Society expects you to follow a formula: find a stable partner from a 'respectable' background, someone who checks all the traditional boxes. But what if your checklist is completely different? What if you are more interested in someone who will stargaze with you or nerd out over 'Game of Thrones' theories than someone who just 'fits' neatly into your family's expectations?

In India, where relationships are often seen as a family affair, introverts and non-conformists can feel like outsiders in their own love lives. Families often evaluate potential matches not just on personal compatibility but on their ability to 'merge' with the extended clan. It is like taking someone out on a date, but instead of a quiet dinner, you are presenting them to a panel of judges who already have a list of criteria. For someone who values privacy or wants to get to know a partner without all that external noise, it is overwhelming, to say the least.

Now, toss in the societal pressure. Whether it is aunties at weddings or random acquaintances on social media, there's no shortage of people who want to know why you are 'still single' or why you are 'not settling down'. It is the kind of exhausting commentary that makes you feel like Raj trying to explain his love life to Howard—it is frustrating, unnecessary, and honestly, none of their business.

But here is the thing: just like Raj and yours truly eventually found love (even after a lot of awkward attempts), you can too. For introverts, it might mean giving yourself permission to take things slow. You do not need a crowd or a flurry of dates; a few meaningful connections are enough. Look for someone who understands that your idea of a perfect evening might be a quiet night watching 'The Planet Earth' series or talking about the mysteries of the universe.

For non-conformists, it is about standing firm in your choices. Do not dim your passions to fit into a traditional box. If you want a partner who will appreciate your love for sci-fi, art, or your eccentricities, make that a priority. There are people out there who will love you because of your quirks, not in spite of them. It might take time, but it is worth holding out for someone who gets that your idea of romance might include gazing at the stars or discussing the poetic brilliance of Tolkien.

And let's not forget, things are changing. More people are realizing that relationships can honor tradition while still making space for individuality. Whether it is introducing your partner to your family when you are ready (not on the first date!) or building connections that grow naturally over time, there's a growing acceptance for blending the old with the new.

The key? Remember that dating is not a test to see how well you fit into societal molds. It is about finding someone who respects both your personality and your values. Your path might not look like everyone else's, and that is okay. Raj did not find love by following anyone else's formula—he found it by staying true to himself, quirks and all.

When I reflect on my own experiences, I had a great time during university, living at home but having a girlfriend. Each time my parents asked the big question, I stalled by replying we were still studying.

During these years, I have seen my parents change from a more traditional approach to becoming milder and accepting that we were two students having a great time together (but still holding onto hope that we would get married). This acceptance of our multicultural bond was their key to avoiding difficult questions from our large family.

So, whether you are an introvert who treasures quiet connections or a non-conformist carving your own path, there's room for you in the world of dating. Take your time, embrace your quirks, and know that the right person will appreciate you for exactly who you are—quirky astrophysics analogies included.

III

Why Finding Love is Different for Introverts, Nerds, and Geeks

Understanding Social Anxiety

Let's talk about social anxiety, that pesky thing that seems to tag along whenever we are faced with social situations—especially in the world of dating. If you are an introvert, a nerd, or a geek, it is like having Rajesh Koothrappali at your side: endearing, awkward, and sometimes unable to say what you really mean. And when it comes to meeting new people, especially people you are interested in, it is like trying to have a heart-to-heart with a brick wall between you and the other person.

For introverts, social anxiety does not mean we are afraid of people or allergic to company. It just means that socializing takes energy—sometimes more energy than we have. Small talk, crowded places, or having to be 'on' all the time can feel exhausting, especially when we know we would be more comfortable in a one-on-one setting. Imagine wanting to have a meaningful conversation but feeling like you are running on fumes the whole time. That is social anxiety at work.

Then there's the added layer of being a nerd or a geek. It is not just that social situations can feel draining; you are doing so while fully aware that your passions—coding, sci-fi, obscure fandoms—are not exactly mainstream conversation starters. It is like walking into a room where everyone's singing pop hits, and all you know is the Star Wars 'cantina' theme. You want to join in, but the fear of being misunderstood keeps you quiet. And that awareness can make social anxiety even worse.

Dating makes this even trickier. Social anxiety turns a first date into a mental chess game. Should you reveal your love for Dungeons & Dragons? Is it too soon to talk about your Marvel marathon? And then there's the aftermath—analyzing every word, every glance, wondering if you came across as 'too much' or 'not enough'.

I can still remember my first date. I was around 18 years old and worked part-time in a supermarket. A beautiful young lady had caught my eye for some weeks. I worked in the aisle with candy and chocolate. She passed by week after week and took the initiative. We went to our first movie! After the movie, we went to a local bar nearby, where we met with some of my friends. They saw how pretty she was and started a conversation with her. At some point that evening, she asked me why I was talking so little. My anxiety turned into embarrassment. It was obvious my friends were trying to flirt with her and actually won the game.

Weeks later, I went to the same bar with some friends; one of them arrived late with my first date by his side. You can imagine my self-esteem took a hit. Apparently, I did not lose her because of the way I looked: 6 feet two inches and, at that time in my life, a relatively athletic build. I lost her because of my inability to say the right words to her. After this experience, I conducted quite a study understanding social anxiety, including training in Neuro-Linguistic Programming years later. Below you will find a thing or two I learned in later years.

When you compare physical dating with online dating, it can feel like both a lifeline and a hurdle. On the plus side, you get to interact at your own pace. You can take your time crafting that perfect first message, find common ground through profiles, and ease into conversations without the pressure of face-to-face interactions right away. You can breathe, think, and respond without the usual social pressures. But there's a catch: online dating has its own social anxiety triggers, too.

For one thing, there's the worry about how you are being perceived. You put yourself out there, sharing bits and pieces of who you are, all while wondering if you are coming across as 'too much' or 'not enough'. Does that profile photo look friendly? Did that message sound confident? Social anxiety kicks in, reminding you of every awkward conversation you have ever had and filling in the blanks with worst-case scenarios.

Then there's the waiting game. You send a message, put yourself out there, and then... nothing. Silence. Did they see it? Did they think it was weird? Social anxiety starts replaying the scene in your head like a bad movie, making you question every word you wrote. It is a bit like trying to hit 'pause' on a train that just keeps moving forward, full of questions, worries, and maybe a little dread.

The funny thing is most of this is happening in our own heads. The other person likely has no idea we are running through these mental gymnastics. They might even be just as anxious. But when social anxiety is part of your dating experience, every step feels like an uphill climb. You're not only trying to connect with someone; you're also managing that little voice in your head that says, "Are you sure you're doing this right?"

For introverts, nerds, and geeks, social anxiety can make dating feel like a minefield. But here is the truth: Meaningful connections do not come from pretending to be someone else; they happen even when we stay true to ourselves—quirks, awkward pauses, and all. The right person will not be scared off because you take a little time to open up or prefer in-depth chats over small talk.

And here is the silver lining: the same things that make us socially anxious also make us great partners. We notice things. We listen. We care about the person in front of us, not just the idea of 'dating'. We are invested in real conversations, in genuine moments that go beyond surface level chatter. Social anxiety might slow us down, but it also makes us more thoughtful, more aware, and sometimes even more compassionate.

So, yes, finding love can feel different for us, and social anxiety might be part of that experience. But that does not mean we are doomed to sit on the sidelines. It means we take a different route, one that values depth, honesty, and the courage to show up as we are—even when it is not easy.

Dealing with Stereotypes

Ah, stereotypes. They are like those annoying pop-up ads that just will not go away, especially if you are an introvert, nerd, or geek trying to find your way in the dating world. The moment people find out you are into things like tech, gaming, sci-fi, or any niche passion, the labels start to pile up. And let's be honest—it gets a bit ridiculous.

Let's take a moment to break down some of the greatest hits in the stereotype playlist. First, there's the classic "introverts are shy and socially awkward". Sure, some of us prefer our quiet corners and solo time, but that does not mean we are hiding out in our basements, terrified of human contact. Introverts just do not thrive in social settings that feel forced or loud. We recharge by spending time alone or with a few close friends. Small talk with strangers at a party? Not our idea of fun. But a deep conversation with someone we click with? Now, that is something we can get behind. Unfortunately, not everyone seems to realize that introversion does not equal antisocial.

And if you happen to be a geek or nerd, the stereotypes really start to pile up. Apparently, we are all supposed to be hunched over computers 24/7, probably wearing glasses taped in the middle, oblivious to anything outside our own little obsessions. Oh, and let's not forget the idea that nerds are only interested in data, facts, and fantasy worlds. Newsflash: we are fully capable of having conversations that go beyond Star Wars trivia (though, let's be real, that is always a great topic).

Here is the thing—these stereotypes can make dating harder than it needs to be. Imagine trying to make a genuine connection while someone's secretly assuming you are one awkward social blunder away from becoming a hermit. Or worse, they see your love for gaming, science fiction, or coding as a sign that you are incapable of 'normal' interests or relationships. It is frustrating and, frankly, a bit outdated.

The issue with stereotypes is that they put us in a box before we have even had a chance to show who we are. They turn our interests into labels and assumptions rather than unique qualities that make us, well, us. And in dating, where the whole point is to connect with someone for who they are, these stereotypes can feel like extra baggage we did not ask to carry.

For introverts, the stereotype can make us feel pressured to 'prove' we are sociable enough, interesting enough, or extroverted enough to date. It can feel like we are constantly being assessed for how well we can fit into a world built for extroverts, one that expects us to be 'on' all the time. The irony? When we are allowed to be ourselves—when we are not pressured to perform or act a certain way—that is when we shine the brightest. Give an introvert a cozy setting, a meaningful topic, and a good listener, and you will find someone who is fully engaged and genuinely interesting.

For nerds and geeks, the stereotypes hit even harder. We are often seen as overly analytical, socially awkward, or just too obsessed with our 'weird' hobbies to function in the real world. But here is the thing: being passionate about something, whether it is comic books, coding, or collecting rare action figures, does not make us one-dimensional. It makes us interesting. It gives us stories to tell, quirks to share, and a depth that goes beyond small talk. A genuine partner will appreciate that passion instead of seeing it as a red flag.

The good news is that not everyone buys into these stereotypes, and there are plenty of people out there who see beyond them. But dealing with stereotypes does mean being prepared to address them—or, at the very least, showing up as your full self despite them. It is about being open to the possibility that the right person will not just tolerate your interests but will actually enjoy learning about them, quirks and all.

In fact, sometimes owning your 'stereotype' can be a great filter. Let's be real—if someone cannot appreciate your love for Doctor Who or your need for quiet downtime, they are probably not the right fit anyway.

Why waste energy pretending to be someone you are not? The beauty of being an introvert, nerd, or geek is that you bring a unique perspective to the table. Sure, we might get excited about things other people find 'weird', but that is what makes us fun. That is what makes us different.

So, here is the plan: instead of letting stereotypes box us in, let's use them as a way to filter out anyone who does not get it.

Embrace that love for comic book lore, that fascination with coding languages, or that need to recharge after socializing. These are not flaws or quirks to hide; they are exactly what makes you, you. Believe it or not, there's someone out there who will see those qualities and think, "Yes, this is exactly the kind of person I've been looking for."

A tip from my personal experience: during my time as a student, I found that playing pool and having a beer with my fellow students was a great way to have genuine conversations with people who understood me and, at the same time, focus on one thing - the pool table - instead of searching for small talk.

My example shows you are not 'just an introvert', or 'just a nerd', or any other label people try to slap on you. As I mentioned in the prologue, no one is 100% introverted or 100% extroverted. You are a whole person with interests, passions, and a unique way of seeing the world. And the right person? They are not just going to tolerate that—they are going to love it!

So, bring your full self to the table, stereotypes be damned. Because if you are going to find someone who really gets you, they are going to have to see beyond the labels. They will need to appreciate you for everything you bring to the relationship: depth, curiosity, loyalty, and yes, maybe a little geekiness, too.

The Power of Authenticity

Let's get one thing straight—there's a lot of advice out there telling us to 'just be yourself'. It is practically a dating mantra, yet somehow, it always feels easier said than done. For introverts, nerds, and geeks, 'being yourself' can feel like a tightrope walk. We are wired to go deeper, to ask the questions others might avoid, to care about things that are not always seen as mainstream. So, when it comes to dating, the idea of showing up as our authentic selves can feel like taking a leap of faith, hoping that whoever's on the other side gets it.

Keep in mind: authenticity is our superpower. It is what makes us stand out. In a world of 'perfect' profiles and endless attempts to be clever or charming, being real is refreshing. It is also what helps us find people who are genuinely right for us. Sure, embracing authenticity might mean showing up with all the quirks, the niche interests, and the social hesitations that make us who we are, but that is exactly the point.

We are not here to impress everyone; we are here to find the one person who appreciates the real deal.

For introverts, authenticity means feeling okay with our need for space and silence. We do not have to pretend to be the life of the party just to fit in. In fact, embracing our quieter side can be a game-changer. It means showing up in a way that is true to us, whether that is through thoughtful conversations, genuine interest, or just being fully present without feeling pressured to 'perform'. When you are authentic about your introversion, you are letting others know that you value depth over noise, and that is a quality that attracts people looking for something more meaningful.

For nerds and geeks, authenticity might look like owning your interests—even the ones people tend to brush off as 'too niche'. If you are passionate about a particular fandom, hobby, or topic, let it shine. The right person will not be put off by your knowledge of comic book lore or your love for coding; they will be intrigued. They will see it as part of what makes you unique, as a glimpse into what you genuinely care about. And while not everyone will get it, that is okay. Authenticity filters out those who are not on the same wavelength and opens the door to people who love that you are unapologetically yourself.

Now, let's be honest—being authentic is not always easy, especially in a dating landscape that often rewards surface level charm over substance. It can be tempting to put up a bit of a front, to smooth over the parts of ourselves we think might be 'too much' or 'too weird'. But think about it: if we are not showing up as ourselves, then the connections we are making are based on a version of us that is not real. And ultimately, that is going to feel empty. Authenticity, while it may feel vulnerable, is what gives relationships a real chance to grow.

One of the best parts about embracing authenticity is that it frees us from the need to constantly impress. When you are real, you are not putting on a show; you are just being. That means there's no need to worry about saying the 'right' thing or fitting into a certain mold. You can relax, show up as you are, and let the right connections unfold naturally. The beauty of authenticity is that it does not rely on tactics or strategies; it relies on trust—trusting that you are enough just as you are and that the right person will see and appreciate that.

When you embrace authenticity, you actually make dating easier for the other person, too. By showing up as yourself, you are giving them permission to do the same. You're setting a tone of honesty, a vibe that says, "I'm here to be real, and I hope you are, too." It takes the pressure off both sides and allows for conversations that go beyond the usual dating small talk.

Suddenly, you are not just two people trying to impress each other - you are two people genuinely getting to know each other.

The truth is, finding love is not about playing a role; it is about finding someone who loves your role in the story of your life. When you are authentic, you are not just opening yourself up to love—you are opening yourself up to the right kind of love. The kind that sees you for who you are, quirks and all, and says, "This is exactly what I was looking for."

So, if you are an introvert, a nerd, or a geek, remember that your authenticity is your strength. It is what makes you unique, and it is what will attract someone who truly values you. Sure, there might be people who do not get it, who see your interests as 'too niche' or your quietness as 'too reserved'. But those people are not your people. Your people will see your authenticity as a breath of fresh air in a world that is often more focused on appearances than depth.

As an IT entrepreneur, I work with many individuals who would qualify as introverts and nerds. I have invented a definition for them: they are my techy soulmates. These soulmates are connected by one superpower, 'authenticity'.

In the end, being authentic is not just about finding love – it is about living in a way that feels true to you and the people who bring positive energy into your life. And when you meet someone who appreciates that, you will know it is not because you fit a certain image or because you played a part. It will be because you showed up as yourself, and they loved you for it.

So go ahead, bring your full self to the table. Share your quirks, passions, and quieter side. Show up as you are, not as who you think you are supposed to be. In the world of dating, authenticity is not just powerful—it is the key to finding the kind of connection that lasts.

IV

The Rise of Online Dating – Opportunities and Challenges

The Growth of Online Dating in India

Let's face it—India is in the midst of a dating revolution. Just a couple of decades ago, the idea of 'meeting someone online' would have raised more than a few eyebrows. The closest thing to online dating might have been those newspaper matrimonials or, if you were lucky, a match arranged by a distant relative who knew a friend's cousin's son. But now, things look very different. Online dating is not just an option; it is become a mainstream way to connect, especially for young Indians looking to find love, companionship or just explore the possibilities.

India's online dating boom did not happen overnight. It has been building for years, thanks to cheaper smartphones, affordable data, and a generation that is more connected to the world than ever. Suddenly, with the internet in almost every hand, a new world of dating opened up. Platforms like Tinder, Bumble, TrulyMadly, and others came flooding in, each offering a way to meet people beyond your immediate social circle, community, or even city. And just like that, dating apps became as familiar as ordering food or booking a cab.

But it is not just about access. The rise of online dating in India reflects a shift in mindset—a move toward individual choice, something that is pretty groundbreaking in a society where marriage is still largely seen as a family affair. For generations, relationships in India were often about aligning families, communities, and cultural expectations. Now, with online dating, people have the freedom to choose their own partners based on mutual interests, personal connection, and compatibility. It is a whole new level of independence that previous generations did not have.

For introverts, nerds, and geeks, this shift is especially meaningful. Online dating offers a way to ease into conversations, take things at a comfortable pace, and avoid the pressure of making an instant impression in person. Gone are the days when you had to rely on family introductions or awkward social setups to meet someone. Now, you can connect based on shared interests, message back-and-forth, and feel the vibe before deciding to meet in person. It is like having a built-in buffer that lets you be yourself without the typical first date pressure.

Of course, this new freedom has also brought its own challenges. For one, the sheer volume of people on dating apps can be overwhelming. It is like standing in a crowd, trying to pick out a friendly face, only now the 'crowd' is millions of profiles, each with its own tagline and carefully curated photos. You find yourself swiping through options faster than you can keep track of, and sometimes it feels like quantity overshadows quality. When every swipe brings a new profile, it is easy to lose sight of the real connections you are looking for.

Another big change in online dating in India is the shift from traditional criteria to personal preferences. In the past, families often looked for matches based on factors like caste, religion, and socioeconomic background. Online dating does not entirely erase these factors, but it gives people the freedom to prioritize personal chemistry over the usual checkboxes. For introverts and people who do not fit the conventional mold, this is huge. It means you can look for someone who gets you, appreciates your interests, and values your personality, rather than just ticking off boxes for family approval.

But with this new freedom comes a certain level of complexity, too. Online dating has its own 'rules', and navigating them can be tricky. For one, there's the unspoken pressure to present the best version of yourself—choosing the right photos, crafting a profile that is both interesting and authentic, and finding the perfect opener. It is like preparing for a first impression, only digitally, and it can be exhausting. For introverts and geeks, this can feel like a bit of a game—one where the real you has to shine through all the polish and filters.

And then there's the infamous 'ghosting' problem. Online dating gives people the option to disappear without a word, leaving conversations (and sometimes emotions) hanging. It is a strange, modern-day phenomenon that feels even more unsettling in a culture where relationships traditionally come with expectations of commitment and respect. Ghosting can be especially rough for those of us who value genuine connections. There's nothing quite like getting excited about a conversation only to see it vanish without explanation.

Despite these challenges, the rise of online dating in India is a game-changer. It is a way for people to explore, to meet others on their own terms, and to take their time finding a connection that feels right. For introverts, it is a way to date without being thrust into social settings that feel unnatural. For geeks, it is a way to lead with interests and passions, letting others see the things that light us up. And for everyone, it is a chance to move beyond the traditional boundaries of caste, community, and geography to explore a wider range of possibilities.

The growth of online dating in India is about more than just swipes and matches; it is about redefining what it means to choose a partner in a way that feels right for you. It is about embracing the opportunity to be real, to look for something genuine, and to find someone who appreciates you for exactly who you are. And yes, it might come with its own ups and downs, but the freedom to explore, connect, and find love on your own terms? That is worth every challenge.

So here we are, in a world where online dating is no longer just a novelty. It is a new chapter in how we think about love, connection, and the kind of relationships we want to build. And for introverts, nerds, geeks, and everyone in between, it is a chance to find a partner who is not just swiping for fun but looking to connect with someone real.

Advantages of Digital Dating for Introverts

For introverts, dating in the traditional sense can sometimes feel like being thrown into the deep end of a crowded pool. You are expected to make small talk, stand out, and somehow make an impression, all while trying not to lose your sanity in a noisy, crowded place. It is a lot. But here is where digital dating steps in and changes the game—especially for those of us who thrive in quieter spaces and prefer meaningful conversations over loud bars and packed parties.

One of the biggest perks of online dating for introverts is that it allows us to set the pace. Unlike in person dating, where there's often this unspoken pressure to be 'on' and keep the conversation flowing, digital dating lets us take things a bit slower. We can spend time crafting a thoughtful message, think about what we actually want to say, and maybe even breathe for a second before responding. In a world that sometimes feels like it is always rushing forward, online dating gives us the chance to slow things down and connect in a way that feels comfortable.

And then there's the beauty of messaging. For introverts, texting and messaging are a kind of superpower. You do not have to worry about filling every pause with words, and there's no pressure to respond immediately. It is perfectly okay to take a moment, collect your thoughts, and reply when you are ready. In fact, messaging actually levels the playing field for introverts—it gives us time to be ourselves without the constant anxiety of saying the 'right' thing in real-time. You can start with a quick, "Hey, I noticed you are into sci-fi. Got a favorite series?" and let the conversation build from there. There is no need for forced small talk or awkward pauses.

Another advantage of digital dating? You get to be selective in a way that feels empowering rather than overwhelming. Swiping might feel a bit strange initially, but it is actually a great way for introverts to explore different personalities without the pressure of face-to-face interactions. You are in control—you decide who you want to connect with, and you can take your time getting to know someone without the awkwardness of a first date right off the bat. For those of us who are a little more cautious about diving into new connections, this 'window-shopping' approach lets us ease into things.

And let's talk about the freedom to lead with our interests. In a typical dating setup, it is not always easy to bring up the things that truly excite us, especially if they are not exactly mainstream. But with online dating, you can choose to highlight your passions right in your profile. Love classic video games? Go ahead and mention it. Prefer a quiet night with a book over a wild night out?

Put it out there. For introverts who want to attract people who genuinely appreciate their hobbies and interests, online dating lets us be upfront about who we are—and attract the kind of people who actually get it.

Digital dating also removes the pressure to meet-up too soon. In traditional dating, you might feel rushed to go on a physical date after just a few conversations, which can be a nightmare for introverts who prefer to build a bit of comfort first. Online dating gives us that flexibility. You can take your time getting to know someone before meeting face-to-face, ensuring there's at least some level of connection established beforehand. It is like getting a preview of what you are signing up for, which can make all the difference when it comes to feeling comfortable.

One often-overlooked benefit of online dating for introverts is the ability to control the environment. We do not have to meet in places that drain our energy. Instead, we get to set up that first meet-up in a way that works for us. If you are someone who thrives in quiet, intimate settings, you can suggest a cozy coffee shop, a peaceful park, or even a casual video call before committing to meeting up in person. There's no pressure to do anything that does not feel right, and you get to ease into dating in a way that is on your terms.

Finally, online dating allows us to weed out the people who do not respect our boundaries. Introverts value their personal space and downtime, and the last thing we want is someone who does not get that. Digital dating gives us the chance to set expectations early on. We can be clear about our need for quieter settings, meaningful conversations, and time to recharge. If someone doesn't respect that? Well, there's no harm done—they are just a swipe away from becoming part of the past.

In a nutshell, online dating opens up new possibilities for introverts, letting us approach dating with less pressure and more control. It is a chance to show up as our true selves, to connect over shared interests, and to take our time finding someone who genuinely appreciates who we are. There is no need to force ourselves into social settings that drain us, no need to pretend to be more outgoing than we are—just the freedom to find love at our own pace, in our own way.

So, while the world of online dating may have its quirks and challenges, it offers something that is invaluable to introverts: the space to be ourselves. And in the world of dating, that is a pretty powerful advantage.

Challenges of the Online Dating World

If there's one thing online dating is not short on, is its challenges. Sure, it opens doors, creates connections, and gives introverts, nerds, and geeks a way to meet people without the usual social circus. But let's be real—digital dating has its own set of hurdles, some of which can feel just as intimidating as those awkward first dates we would rather avoid. For every advantage, there's a new puzzle to solve. And while some of these challenges can be shrugged off, others can make online dating feel a bit like navigating a maze with hidden traps.

First off, let's talk about profile pressure. Online dating starts with creating a profile—a few photos, a catchy bio, maybe a list of your favorite interests. Sounds easy enough, right? But for those of us who are not naturally inclined to put ourselves out there, this process can feel overwhelming. How do you summarize your entire personality in a few lines? How do you convey your sense of humor, love for sci-fi, and introverted nature without sounding like you are trying too hard? It is a bit like writing a resume, except this time, it is your love life on the line.

Imagine Rajesh Koothrappali agonizing over his bio. Does he highlight his love for astrophysics, or does that sound too niche? Should he include his obsession with Star Wars, or will that scare people off? After much overthinking, he ends up with: "Astrophysicist. Poet. Lover of all things intergalactic. Swipe right if you can name my favorite constellation." Charming? Absolutely. But the process probably took him three hours and a full cup of tea.

And then there's the photo dilemma. You want to look approachable but not like you are trying too hard. You want to highlight your personality but still keep things natural. For introverts, this can be especially tricky because, let's be honest, many of us do not love being in front of the camera in the first place.

Once you have conquered the profile, there's the challenge of swiping. Swiping might seem simple at first, but it can quickly turn into a mind-numbing exercise. You are faced with an endless stream of profiles, and it is all too easy to get caught up in the game of left and right, yes and no. It is fast-paced, sometimes overwhelming, and can leave you feeling like you are looking for a needle in a haystack. For introverts and people who prefer meaningful connections over quick judgments, swiping can feel exhausting—like speed dating on steroids.

Another tricky part of online dating is dealing with the superficial side of it. Let's face it: online dating often places a lot of emphasis on appearances and quick judgments. Profiles flash by, bios get skimmed, and sometimes it feels like people are more interested in 'likes' than getting to know someone. For those who value depth and connection, this swipe-based approach can feel shallow. It is easy to get discouraged when it seems like everyone's looking for something casual or unwilling to take the time to get to know the real you.

Then there's the issue of 'choice overload'. With so many options at your fingertips, it is easy to feel like you are always on the lookout for someone 'better'. You match with someone interesting, but before you can fully invest, there's another profile and then another. This abundance of choices can make it hard to focus on one person, leaving people feeling like they are constantly missing out on something—or someone. For those of us who prefer a more focused, deliberate approach to dating, this endless stream of potential matches can feel more like a distraction than an opportunity.

Another challenge that often goes unspoken is managing expectations. It is all too easy to get excited when you match with someone, picturing where things might go and building a bit of a story in your mind. However, online dating does not always lead to perfect connections. Sometimes conversations fizzle out, and other times, meeting in person does not quite match the vibe you felt online. It can be disappointing, even frustrating, to put energy into something only to feel like you are back at square one. For introverts and people who value quality over quantity, these letdowns can start to feel exhausting after a while.

And let's not forget the security aspect. While dating apps have made it easier than ever to meet people, they also come with risks. There's always a small voice in the back of our minds reminding us to be cautious—to verify that the person on the other end is who they say they are. For those of us who value trust and safety, navigating the online dating world can sometimes feel like walking on eggshells, balancing curiosity and caution in equal measure.

Despite its quirks and pitfalls, online dating offers opportunities that simply did not exist before. It may not be perfect, but it provides a platform to connect, explore, and even thrive on your own terms. The key is approaching it with a sense of balance—appreciate the possibilities, but keep your expectations grounded. After all, online dating is just a tool, and like any tool, it is how you use it that makes the difference.

Yes, there will be challenges. You might face awkward conversations, deal with the sting of ghosting, or navigate mismatched connections. But here is the thing: those bumps in the road do not define your journey—they are just part of it. Even Rajesh, after all his missteps and overthinking, never gives up on the idea of connection. His resilience reminds us that each awkward interaction or unreturned message is simply a step toward finding something meaningful.

There is an ancient Latin saying: 'per aspera ad astra,' which means 'through hardship to the stars.' So, whenever an obstacle arises that seems to block your path, in reality, the obstacle has an essential function. This function forces us introverts who struggle to find their soulmate to become better each time. Better in conversations, handling social pressure, and becoming more conscious of who we are to become the best version of ourselves.

So, take a deep breath. Approach each swipe, each message, with curiosity and openness. Sure, not every interaction will be a winner, but every experience—good or bad—brings you closer to finding the connection that feels right for you. And if Raj can keep trying, quirks and all, so can you.

V

Crafting the Perfect Profile – How to Stand Out Authentically

Building a Strong Profile Foundation

I briefly explained how to create a social media profile in the previous chapter. In this chapter, we will dive deep into how to create your perfect dating profile.

You have got a few lines, a couple of pictures, and just enough space to give people a snapshot of who you are—no pressure, right? Building a dating profile can be daunting for introverts, nerds, geeks, and anyone who is not thrilled about self-promotion. But here is the good news: you do not have to be flashy or over-the-top to stand out. In fact, the most effective profiles are the ones that feel real and relatable. It is all about setting up a foundation that shows off the real you without trying to fit into someone else's mold.

Think of your profile as the opening scene of a movie about you. It does not have to tell the whole story, but it should give people a sense of what makes you interesting, unique, and worth getting to know. Start with the basics—what parts of your personality do you want to put forward? Are you a quiet thinker with a quirky sense of humor? An outdoorsy bookworm who loves a good sci-fi series? The goal is to show a little slice of who you are, something genuine that gives people a reason to pause and think, "Hey, I'd like to know more."

When building your profile foundation, keep it simple and straightforward. Start with a few lines that give a sense of your personality without going overboard. Imagine you are talking to a friend who is introducing you to someone new. You would not go into a lengthy backstory, but you would share a few key details. For example, something like, 'Introvert who loves cooking, books, and late-night movie marathons', tells people a lot about you in a single line. Or, if you are a techie with a love for old-school gaming, try something like, 'Software developer by day, retro gamer by night—currently on a mission to finish every Zelda game.' These small touches make your profile feel specific to you, which is the first step toward standing out.

One of the biggest mistakes people make is trying too hard to be 'clever' or 'cool'. If that is naturally you, great! But if you are just throwing in lines that do not really represent who you are, it can end up sounding forced.

People can tell when a profile feels authentic versus when it feels like an attempt to grab attention. The reality is that being genuine is a lot more appealing than being over-the-top. So, instead of writing what you think people want to hear, write what feels true to you.

Next up: photos. Now, I know this can be a tricky part, especially if you are not someone who loves being in front of a camera. But the goal here is not to look like a model or create a highlight reel; it is to give people a glimpse of your everyday life. Choose a few photos that reflect who you are in real life. If you are the outdoorsy type, maybe a photo of you on a hike or at a beautiful scenic spot. If you are a bookworm, a picture of you at your favorite cozy reading spot can say a lot without words. The idea is to show what you genuinely enjoy rather than just trying to look impressive.

Avoid group photos or overly filtered images—while they might seem tempting, they can actually make it harder for people to get a sense of you. And if you are hesitant to put yourself out there, remember that you do not need a ton of photos. Two or three solid shots that capture who you are is all you really need. Think of your photos as little windows into your life, showing people the version of you they would get to know if you spent time together.

Another foundational element to consider is your profile bio—the space where you can share a bit more detail about what makes you tick. If you are not sure where to start, try focusing on the things you are passionate about. Mention your interests, hobbies, or the things you would genuinely love to do with a partner. For instance, if you are a fan of sci-fi movies, say so! Or, if you have been dreaming about a road trip through the mountains, mention it. The right person will appreciate those specifics, and they might even share your interests.

A great bio also has a mix of fun and substance. You want to be approachable and relatable but also give a bit of insight into what you are looking for. Try something like, "Coffee enthusiast who never says no to a good movie marathon. Looking for someone who doesn't mind a little quiet time and enjoys exploring new places—bonus points if you can teach me something new." It is light, open, and specific enough to attract people who vibe with your interests.

And here is a pro tip: include a question or two in your bio to encourage conversation. It can be as simple as "Favorite book of all time?" or "What's one place you'd love to visit?" This not only makes it easier for people to reach out but also gives them a starting point that's more engaging than a generic "hi."

When it comes to building your profile foundation, the most important thing is to focus on what makes you feel comfortable and authentic. You do not have to pretend to be more outgoing, adventurous, or anything than you are. Think of this profile as a way to connect with the kind of person who appreciates you for who you are. Because when it comes down to it, a strong profile foundation is less about attracting everyone and more about finding someone who genuinely gets you.

Building an authentic profile does not have to be complicated. With a few thoughtful choices, you can create a profile that speaks to who you are without trying too hard. After all, the whole point is to meet someone who will like you for the real you—the introvert, the nerd, the gamer, the thinker. So, start with a foundation that feels true, and let the right person find you from there.

Showcasing Your Interests and Values

This is your opportunity to move beyond the basics and show people what makes you, well, you. It is not just about listing hobbies or personality traits—it is about giving a glimpse of what lights you up and what you stand for. The best part? The right people will appreciate you all the more for it.

Think about one of my beloved characters, Sheldon Cooper, crafting his dating profile for The Big Bang Theory's online matchmaking experiment. You can almost see him agonizing over whether to include his love for trains, his obsession with flags, or his spot on the couch as part of his 'values'.

Of course, Sheldon being Sheldon, he would probably write something like: "Physicist with a passion for order, organization, and all things logical. Looking for someone who understands the sanctity of designated seating and enjoys debating scientific theories over dinner." And as quirky as that sounds, it is authentic—it shows exactly who he is and invites someone with similar interests (or patience for his quirks) to connect.

My tip for you: do not be afraid to get specific. Saying you "like movies" is fine, but saying you are a fan of classic sci-fi or that you never miss a Marvel premiere? Now, that is something people can connect with.

The key is to mention details that show a little piece of who you are. If you are a die-hard Star Wars fan or you are obsessed with '80s arcade games, put it out there. You're not trying to attract everyone; you're looking for people who think, "Hey, me too!" or who are at least intrigued by what you love.

And remember, it is not just about interests—it is also about values. What really drives you? Maybe you are passionate about environmental causes, or you volunteer regularly. These are not just nice 'extras' on your profile; they are part of who you are. If kindness, honesty, or curiosity are things you value in yourself and others, go ahead and mention them. These details help paint a picture of what you bring to a relationship and the type of person you would like to find.

When describing your interests, try not to make it sound like a laundry list. Instead, give a little context. If you love cooking, talk about your favorite dish to make or a recipe you are perfecting. If you are into gaming, maybe mention your current obsession or the game that got you hooked in the first place. This approach not only makes your profile more engaging but also gives people something specific to connect with or ask you about.

One thing to avoid? Overthinking. It is easy to fall into the trap of trying to craft the 'perfect' profile, but the truth is that authenticity is far more attractive than perfection.

Do not worry about sounding impressive; focus on being real. If you love cheesy action movies or have a soft spot for board games, say so! These little quirks are what make you interesting, and they will help the right people feel drawn to you.

Another way to showcase your interests is to mention how you like to spend your time. Instead of just listing 'hiking' as an interest, for example, talk about why you love it: the quiet, the fresh air, the challenge of reaching the summit. Or, if you are a book lover, share your favorite genres or a book that is had an impact on you. Letting people in on why you love what you love adds depth to your profile and gives a sense of who you are beyond the surface.

It is also okay to mention the kind of activities you would like to do with a partner. Think about what would make you happy in a relationship. Maybe it is cozy movie nights, museum visits, or road trips with a good playlist. Sharing these small hopes or 'date goals' can help people picture what life might look like with you and give them an idea of the kind of relationship you are seeking. It is subtle but goes a long way in showing that you are not just looking to meet someone—you are looking to share experiences that mean something to you.

Do not be shy about putting a bit of humor or personality into how you showcase your interests. If you're a coffee addict, try something like, "Fueling my life one espresso at a time." If you are a bit of a homebody, "Happiest with a good book and a cozy blanket" can say it all. Adding personality helps break the ice and makes you feel more approachable. And for those of us who might not love chatting with strangers, this kind of openness in a profile can make that first conversation a little easier.

Showcasing your interests and values is not about putting on a show; it is about showing what matters to you. It helps the right people see you for who you really are and makes it easier for them to start a natural conversation. When you are upfront about what you love and what you believe in, you are inviting someone to get to know the real you. And in a world of dating profiles that sometimes all sound the same, that authenticity is what makes you stand out.

Even Sheldon eventually found someone who valued his quirks rather than tolerating them. Amy did not just accept his love for trains or his need for a specific bathroom schedule—she appreciated them as part of who he was. That is the kind of connection you are looking for—someone who not only gets you but celebrates you.

So go ahead—share what you are into, what you care about, and even the little quirks that make you, you. Because when it comes down to it, the right person isn't looking for someone 'perfect'. They are looking for someone genuine, someone they can relate to, and someone who just might love what they love.

Setting Expectations Clearly

Let's face it—dating can get complicated when people are not on the same page. And online dating, with all its options and the occasional mixed signals, only amplifies this. That is why setting expectations clearly in your profile is not just helpful; it is essential. Think of it as a way to let people know what you are looking for without leaving them guessing. Being upfront does not just save you time; it makes it easier to find someone who is genuinely aligned with what you want.

Take Leonard and Penny from 'The Big Bang Theory', for example. Leonard is all-in from the start, hoping for a serious relationship, while Penny is hesitant and unsure about commitment. If Leonard had been upfront about his intentions early on, it might have saved both of them some emotional turbulence. Of course, it all works out in the end, but their mismatched expectations caused plenty of tension along the way. The lesson? Clear communication makes everything smoother—both in sitcoms and in real life.

So, what does 'setting expectations' actually look like? It does not mean you need to lay out your life plan in bullet points. Instead, think of it as sharing your intentions, the kind of connection you are hoping to build, and what you value in a relationship. Whether you are looking for something casual, a meaningful connection, or even a long-term partnership, being clear about it will attract people who are on the same wavelength and filter out those who are not.

Let's start with a simple, straightforward approach. If you are looking for something serious, say so! You could add a line like, "Looking for a real connection that could lead to something meaningful." It is open, honest, and sends a clear message without feeling heavy. Or, if you're more focused on meeting someone to share good times with and see where things go, try something like, "Hoping to find someone fun to share new experiences with—open to wherever it leads." The idea is to let people know where your head is so there are no surprises.

Now, if you are someone who values certain qualities in a partner, do not be afraid to mention them. Maybe kindness and curiosity are must-haves for you, or you are looking for someone who appreciates quiet nights in just as much as the occasional adventure. Including these in your profile is not about creating a checklist but attracting people who resonate with your values and lifestyle. A simple line like, "Looking for someone who values honesty and a good laugh" or "I am drawn to people who are thoughtful and genuine" says a lot without coming across as demanding.

Another key part of setting expectations is discussing what kind of relationship dynamic you enjoy. This does not have to be complicated. Are you looking for a partner who enjoys shared activities, like movie marathons or hiking, or someone who respects your need for personal space and independence? Mentioning these preferences in a natural way can give people a sense of how a relationship with you might look. For example, "I'm all about finding someone who loves a good Netflix binge and respects quiet nights in" or "Hoping to find a partner who values balance—a mix of together time and personal time."

A common misconception is that being clear about your expectations might appear rigid or demanding. But the truth is, it is actually refreshing. In a world of profiles that often say very little, knowing what someone's looking for can feel like a breath of fresh air. It is not about limiting yourself or coming off as 'picky'; it is about letting the right people know that you are serious about finding someone who truly aligns with what you want.

One of the best ways to keep things light while setting expectations is to approach it with a little humor or personality. Instead of saying, "Not interested in games", try something like, "Looking for someone who knows what they want—bonus points if it's pizza on a Friday night." It is playful but gets the message across. If you are hoping to avoid endless swiping and want something genuine, a line like, "Not here for endless chats—hoping for a real connection." can set the tone without sounding overly serious.

And finally, remember that setting expectations does not mean boxing yourself in. It is okay to keep things open-ended or flexible. If you are unsure of exactly what you want but know the kind of energy you are looking for, say that! Try something like, "Open to where things go, but hoping for something that feels real" or "Looking for someone I click with—let's see where it leads." This approach lets people know that you are open to possibilities while still seeking a meaningful connection.

Setting expectations is really just a way to be honest, to invite the kind of connections that align with your values and intentions. It might feel a bit vulnerable at first, but it is actually one of the best things you can do for yourself. You are creating a profile that attracts people who appreciate your clarity, honesty, and openness. And at the end of the day, isn't that the kind of person you want to attract?

So, as you write your profile, take a moment to consider what you are truly looking for and let that come through in your words. Not everyone will be a match, and that is the beauty of it. By setting clear expectations, you are giving yourself a better chance of finding someone who is genuinely right for you—and is not that the whole point?

VI
The Art of Conversation – Starting and Sustaining Meaningful Interactions

Starting Engaging Conversations

Starting a conversation on a dating app can feel like a delicate dance. You want to make a good impression, keep it casual, and ideally spark something interesting—all without sounding like you are trying too hard. For introverts, nerds, geeks, or anyone who thrives on genuine connections rather than small talk, kicking things off meaningfully is key. The goal is not to wow someone with clever lines or charm them right out of the gate but to create a natural opening for a real, engaging conversation.

Let's begin with the basics: the opening line. Sure, a simple "Hey" or "How's it going?" can technically start a conversation, but it does not really offer much to work with. Instead, try something that shows you have actually taken an interest in the other person's profile. Maybe they have mentioned a love for hiking, a favorite book, or a shared fandom. Lead with that! A message like, "I noticed you're into hiking—got a favorite trail?" or "Saw you're a fellow Star Wars fan—Jedi or Sith?" does more than just say hello; it invites them to talk about something they care about.

For me, finding the right way to connect was not always easy. As I mentioned earlier in this book, I lost my first date to a friend simply because I was not saying much. She had asked me out, and I thought showing up was enough. Spoiler: it was not. That night, my friends ended up chatting with her more than I did, and before I knew it, she was dating one of them. I realized I needed to approach conversations differently—without trying to be someone I was not.

Instead of diving into flirty banter, which was not my strength, I leaned into what I was comfortable with. I started taking dates to movies and ended the night at a pool hall. That way, we had an activity to focus on, and I did not feel pressured to come up with clever lines. Conversations flowed naturally, talking about the movie, laughing over missed shots at the pool table, and gradually opening up about our interests. Every date became an opportunity to learn more about myself and what worked for me.

This 'slow build' approach is something I would recommend to anyone who feels a bit shy about starting conversations. You do not have to jump into heavy topics right away. A relaxed, steady flow can be just as effective. Start with something simple, like the movie you just watched together or weekend plans, and gradually work your way to more meaningful questions as you both feel comfortable.

Another approach to keep things engaging is to keep a little bit of curiosity in your tone. Show interest in their experiences, opinions, and perspectives. People love to talk about themselves, especially when they feel that the other person is genuinely curious. Even a simple, "I would love to hear more about that" can turn a casual conversation into something that feels more meaningful. Remember, the goal is to make the other person feel heard and valued—not just to keep the conversation moving along.

And do not be afraid to share a little about yourself, too. It does not have to be a life story, but a small detail can make a big difference. If they mention a favorite movie, you could respond with, "I have been meaning to watch that one! My go-to is usually a classic action flick, though. Got any recommendations?" By sharing something about yourself, you are letting them see a glimpse of your personality, which can help the conversation feel balanced and reciprocal.

Humor is another great tool, especially if it comes naturally to you. A playful question like, "Serious debate—pineapple on pizza: yes, or no?" can spark laughter and ease the pressure. And do not underestimate the power of genuine compliments. Saying something like, "Your travel photos look amazing! Any tips for Italy?" or "That painting hobby sounds incredible—do you have a favorite style?" shows that you are paying attention to more than just appearances.

Finally, be mindful of pace. Sometimes, taking a beat before responding can feel more genuine than rushing to reply. It gives both of you time to think and adds a natural rhythm to the conversation.

For me, this one is tricky since my speed of speech is quite high, especially when I am nervous. I learned to control this and slow down my pace by using breathing techniques. I am sure that, as my fellow introvert, my readers will have no issues finding these techniques online. If not, please visit my website with more tips and tricks for introverts.

In the end, starting an engaging conversation is all about setting a comfortable, authentic tone. The aim is not to impress but to connect—to find those small moments where you both feel heard, appreciated, and intrigued. With the right mix of curiosity, openness, and a dash of humor, you can create conversations that feel as natural as catching up with an old friend, even if you have only just met.

So, take your time, keep it real, and remember that the best conversations are the ones where you can both be yourselves. If you are a bit like me, shy by nature, stay close to yourself, listen to your partner's interests, and discover together if you share common ground. If not, you at least had a great night with a movie and maybe some pool games!

Keeping Conversations Flowing

So, you have passed the icebreaker stage and started a conversation. Now comes the tricky part—keeping it going. There will be a moment when enough has been said about that movie you just watched and how you liked shooting pool for the first time.

For us introverts, nerds, and geeks, sustaining a conversation without it fizzling out can feel like walking a tightrope. Small talk gets dull fast, and there's only so much "How was your day?" you can handle before things start to feel flat. But with a few simple approaches, you can keep conversations flowing in a way that feels real and, better yet, enjoyable.

One of the best ways to keep the conversation alive is by striking a good balance between sharing and listening. Think of it as a friendly game of tennis—you hit the ball over, let them respond, and then it is back to you. When they share something about themselves, whether it is a favorite hobby or a recent experience, show interest by asking more about it and then add a bit of your own perspective. Say they mention they love hiking; you could reply, "That sounds awesome! I have always wanted to try hiking but have not taken the plunge yet. Any tips for a total newbie?" This not only keeps things flowing, but it shows you are engaged without making it all about you.

Another trick? Build on topics they have already shared instead of hopping from one subject to the next. Let's say they mention a love for classic movies. Instead of just moving on to another question, ask them what draws them to that era or if they have a favorite director. It keeps the conversation from feeling like a Q&A and gives it a natural, more relaxed rhythm—more like the conversations we have with friends we are genuinely curious about.

If you are stumped on what to ask, remember that open-ended questions are your best friends. They give people room to share, with no pressure to be concise. Questions like, "What's something you're super into right now?" or "If time wasn't an issue, what hobby would you love to try?" allow them to expand and show a little more about who they are. For introverts, open-ended questions are especially useful because they let the other person lead while you enjoy getting to know them at a comfortable pace.

Let's talk about humor, too. Humor is a fantastic way to keep things light and fun, but it is all about finding the right moment. Think of it like seasoning; a sprinkle here and there is just enough. If they mention a guilty pleasure TV show, for example, you could respond with, "Your secret's safe with me—we all have one show we can't resist." It is a playful way to add personality without taking things off track, showing you are here for a good time but also paying attention to what they are sharing.

What worked for me was my love for two great shows, 'The Big Bang Theory' and 'Friends'. I grew up in the Netherlands, where these shows were a big hit. When I started, there was enough to discuss that night! I can imagine Indian classics like 'Sholay' work well, too, or famous actors like Amitabh Bachchan. As a guy with roots in India growing up in Europe, even with my introverted character, I had two worlds I could choose from.

Knowing when to keep things light and when to go deeper is all about picking up cues. If they are sharing something meaningful, it is best to stay in that vibe rather than rushing to lighten things up. You do not have to steer the conversation back to jokes just because there's a bit of weight to the topic. Often, these more personal, deeper moments are where real connections happen. So, take your time; not every moment needs to be upbeat.

Another great tip? Avoid those 'conversation killers' like one-word answers or flat responses. "Haha, nice" or "Cool" can shut things down fast. Instead, put a little thought into your responses. If they share a funny story about their pet, don't just say, "Cute!"—ask something like, "Does your cat have any other quirky habits?" or "Sounds like a character—what's the funniest thing they've done lately?" That little bit of effort shows you are genuinely engaged, and it keeps the energy of the conversation flowing.

If you sense the conversation slowing, sometimes it helps to throw in a new, fun question or a little 'thought experiment'. Something like, "If you could invite any three people, dead or alive, to dinner, who would you pick?" or

"What's your favorite Bollywood movie?" Questions like these not only reignite the conversation but give both of you a peek into each other's interests and imagination, making things feel a lot less scripted.

Keeping a conversation going is not about having a list of questions or always knowing the perfect thing to say. It is about being curious, engaged, and real. The best conversations flow because both people are interested and invested, letting things unfold at their own pace. So, keep things balanced, stay genuinely curious, and remember that the best conversations are not rehearsed. This lesson of keeping conversations has not been easy for me. A lesson I finally mastered after years of practice!

Transitioning to Deeper Connections

So, you have got the conversation flowing, congratulations! Now comes the part that can feel a little intimidating: taking things to a deeper level. For introverts, nerds, and geeks, this is often where we shine. Surface level small talk, like in that pool hall, has its place, but meaningful conversations are where connections are truly made.

The key to transitioning from light banter to deeper discussions is to let things evolve naturally. Think of it as peeling back layers rather than diving straight to the core. There's no need to jump into heavy topics right away. Instead, look for moments where a topic naturally invites a bit more thought or reflection. For example, if they mention a place they have always wanted to visit, ask what draws them there or what they hope to experience.

These kinds of questions invite depth without feeling forced or overly intense.

A great way to start deepening a connection is by sharing a bit more about yourself—something beyond the basics. This does not mean launching into your life story but offering small insights into your passions or values. For instance, if they ask what you do for work, you might say, "I'm in software development, but I love it because it feels like solving puzzles every day." By giving a glimpse of what drives you, you create an opening for them to respond with more than a polite acknowledgment.

When asking questions, focus on the "why" behind their answers to spark richer conversations. If they mention volunteering, ask what inspired them to get involved. Or if they talk about loving a certain book, ask what makes it their favorite. Questions like these encourage people to share more about their values and experiences, turning a casual chat into something meaningful.

One important tip: listen closely and respond thoughtfully. If they mention something personal—like a recent accomplishment or challenge—show genuine interest. For example, "That sounds like a big win! What was the most rewarding part for you?" Acknowledging these details shows you are engaged and invested in the conversation.

Shared experiences are another powerful way to build depth. If they bring up a passion or hobby you share, dive in! If they love gaming and so do you, discuss what it is about that world that fascinates you both. If they talk about travel, swap dream destinations. Finding these points of connection creates a shared narrative and lays the foundation for more meaningful exchanges.

Humor can also be a fantastic bridge to deeper connections. A light, playful comment can make a conversation feel more relaxed and enjoyable. For example, if they mention a guilty pleasure TV show, you might respond with, "We all have one—mine's an embarrassing addiction to reality cooking competitions." Humor fosters intimacy without making things too serious, keeping the energy balanced.

Cultural nuances are another great conversation layer. Growing up in the Netherlands, I realized my love for tech was seen as 'geeky', while in other cultures, it was considered prestigious. Sharing these insights about your background and experiences can invite the other person to reflect on their own, adding a deeper, personal touch to the discussion.

Vulnerability also plays a role in building intimacy. You do not have to dive into your deepest fears, but mentioning something like, "I have always been a bit nervous about public speaking" or "I cannot help but overanalyze things sometimes" makes you relatable and approachable. Vulnerability creates a sense of trust and openness, showing that you are not just putting on a front.

Finally, remember that not every moment needs to be filled with words. Pauses, when they occur naturally, can be powerful. Letting a silence sit after someone shares something meaningful shows you are absorbing what they have said. It also gives both of you space to reflect, making the conversation feel richer and more authentic.

Deepening a conversation is not about rushing or trying too hard. It is about following the flow, being genuinely curious, and showing that you are open to seeing the real person in front of you. With the right balance of curiosity, humor, and vulnerability, you will find yourself moving into conversations that feel natural, meaningful, and memorable, qualities that form the foundation for real connections.

VII

Choosing the Right Platform – Where to Find Your Perfect Match

Exploring Popular Dating Platforms in India

If you are like most people stepping into the world of online dating, it might feel like walking into a giant buffet. There are tons of options, and each one claims to be 'the best' or 'perfect for everyone'. But here is the reality: not every dating platform will suit every person. Choosing the right one depends on what you are looking for, your personality, and even how much energy you have to put into dating.

Let's take a tour of some of the most popular dating platforms in India. Whether you are looking for a serious relationship, some casual chats, or just curious to see who is out there, there's likely a platform that fits your style. Here, we'll break down a few of the major ones so you can make a choice that is right for you.

1. Tinder: The "GoTo" for Just About Everyone

Tinder is pretty much the first name you hear when people talk about dating apps, and it is easy to see why. With its famous swiperightorleft feature, Tinder lets you browse quickly, giving you the chance to check out a lot of profiles in a short amount of time. If you are someone who likes variety and the chance to meet all kinds of people, this could be a good fit.

- What It is Known For: Tinder is often seen as a casual dating app, but it is not limited to just that. You will find people looking for everything from casual chats to serious relationships. It is a bit of a mixed bag, which means you will need to sift through profiles to find someone whose intentions align with yours.
- Who Might Enjoy It: If you are openminded, enjoy a fastpaced app, and like to chat with different types of people, Tinder offers plenty of options. Just remember that while you can find genuine connections, the vibe on Tinder can sometimes lean towards casual or shortterm dating.
- Things to Keep in Mind: Because Tinder's user base is so big, you might find yourself going through a lot of matches to find someone who clicks. It is easy to feel a bit overwhelmed, so do not be afraid to take breaks or be selective about who you swipe right on.

Tip: Tinder's free version works fine, but if you are serious about finding matches faster, the paid versions offer features like 'Rewind' (to undo a swipe) and 'Passport' (to see people in other locations).

2. Bumble: Where Women Make the First Move

Bumble is a bit of a gamechanger in the dating world because it gives women control over who they talk to. After a match, only the woman can send the first message, which can help cut down on unwanted messages and give a more respectful vibe to the conversations.

- What It is Known For: Bumble is known for its 'womenfirst' approach, which can create a more respectful environment. It also has options for networking (Bumble Bizz) and friendship (Bumble BFF), so if you are looking to expand your social circle beyond dating, it is worth exploring.
- Who Might Enjoy It: If you are an introverted woman who sometimes feels overwhelmed by too many messages, Bumble might feel like a breath of fresh air. For men, it can be a good platform if you are interested in meeting women who are confident and know what they want.
- Things to Keep in Mind: On Bumble, you will need to be active, as matches expire in 24 hours if no message is sent. This can help keep things moving, but if you are someone who likes to take your time, it may feel a bit fastpaced.

Tip: Bumble's 'Spotlight' feature (a paid feature) can boost your profile temporarily, making it visible to more users, which can be helpful if you want to increase your matches quickly.

3. Hinge: "Designed to Be Deleted"

Hinge markets itself as an app "designed to be deleted", aiming at people who want real, lasting relationships. The focus here is on building genuine connections, and profiles offer more detail than on most other platforms. Hinge also uses prompts and questions to encourage meaningful conversations right from the start.

- What It is Known For: Hinge is all about creating a meaningful connection. The prompts and questions allow you to get a sense of someone's personality and values even before you message them. It is popular with people who are looking for something more than just casual dating.
- Who Might Enjoy It: If you are someone who prefers slower, more thoughtful interactions and values compatibility over just looks, Hinge might feel like a natural fit. It is especially appealing to those who are tired of the endless swiping and want something that feels more intentional.
- Things to Keep in Mind: Because Hinge encourages more indepth profiles, you might spend a bit more time reading and responding. But if you are ready to invest in finding a serious connection, this can be a plus rather than a drawback.

Tip: Hinge's 'Standouts' feature shows profiles the app thinks you will be most interested in based on your activity. It is a good way to find compatible matches without endless browsing.

4. OkCupid: Focused on Compatibility

OkCupid has been around for a while and is known for its indepth profiles and emphasis on compatibility. The app uses a series of questions to assess what you are looking for, what you value, and how you approach life, then matches you with people who align with your answers. If you are looking for depth, this is a platform that lets you get to know someone well before you even start chatting.

- What It is Known For: OkCupid is all about compatibility. The app's questions cover everything from values to lifestyle choices, and it uses your answers to give you a compatibility percentage with other users. This makes it easier to find people who share your views and interests.
- Who Might Enjoy It: If you are the type who enjoys a bit of introspection and values a solid compatibility match, OkCupid could be a great fit. The questions are often interesting, and you will get a sense of people's values and personalities before you even match.
- Things to Keep in Mind: OkCupid is a bit more detailed than some other apps, so it may take a little time to set up your profile. But if you are serious about finding someone compatible, it can be worth the investment.

Tip: Answer as many questions as you can honestly. The more you answer, the better the app will be at showing you profiles that match your personality and values.

5. TrulyMadly: Designed with India in Mind

TrulyMadly is specifically tailored to the Indian dating scene, with features that focus on building trust and security for users. It is one of the few dating apps that are built around safety and cultural sensitivities, making it a solid option if you are looking to meet people in India with similar backgrounds.

- What It is Known For: TrulyMadly has a trustbased approach, using 'trust scores' to verify users' identities and weed out fake profiles. This is great if you are concerned about safety and want a platform with a more serious vibe.
- Who Might Enjoy It: If you are looking for a platform that feels rooted in Indian values while allowing you to meet a wide range of people, TrulyMadly could be the right choice. It tends to attract people looking for something more serious and culturally aligned.
- Things to Keep in Mind: The app does require more verification than others, so be prepared to go through the setup process. However, this is a positive if safety and genuine profiles are important to you.

Tip: Build up your trust score by completing the verification steps. This helps you connect with others who are also committed to safety and authenticity.

There's no onesizefitsall when it comes to dating apps. Each platform has its vibe, strengths, and community. It is all about finding the one that suits your personality, comfort level, and what you are hoping to get out of the experience. Remember, online dating should feel enjoyable, not exhausting. Take your time, explore what feels right for you, and do not be afraid to try a few before settling on one that feels like a good fit.

Pro Tip: Start with one or two platforms that align with what you are looking for. Avoid downloading everything at once, as that can get overwhelming quickly. Give each one a fair shot and see which feels most natural.

Remember, I am here to help if you ever need more tips or insights. Feel free to reach out on techysoulmates.com with any questions or suggestions. I would love to hear about your experiences and help however I can. Happy swiping, matching, and connecting—your perfect match could be just a few clicks away!

Niche Platforms for Specific Interests

Sometimes, finding the right dating platform is not just about choosing the one everyone else is on; it is about finding a space where you feel at home, where your passions are not just accepted but shared and celebrated. This is where niche dating platforms come in. These are the communities built around specific interests or unique identities, designed to connect people who 'get it'. Whether you are a gamer, a book lover, or just someone who enjoys the more 'niche' things in life, these platforms can be a gamechanger in helping you meet people on your wavelength.

Here, we'll explore some of the popular niche platforms out there, why they might be a great fit for you, my fellow introvert, and how they can lead to connections that feel natural and, let's be honest, a lot more interesting.

1. For Gamers: Kippo and LFGdating

If you are a gamer, you know how powerful it can be to connect over a shared love of games. Whether you are into MMORPGs, firstperson shooters, or casual mobile games, finding someone who understands the thrill of that next level, or the excitement of a new release can make a world of difference. Enter platforms like Kippo and LFGdating. These dating apps are designed for gamers, with features that let you show off your gaming interests and find people who enjoy the same games as you do.

- Why It Works: On these platforms, you do not have to explain or downplay your love for gaming. It is actually the main attraction. Kippo, for example, lets you build a profile that highlights your favorite games, gaming style, and personality. The profiles feel less like a job interview and more like a fun way to show who you really are.
- Who It's For: If you find yourself more excited about spending Saturday night in a virtual world than at a loud party, or if you've ever said, "Just one more level!" this could be the right space for you. These platforms

attract people who understand the gaming lifestyle and the need for someone who 'gets' it.

· Things to Keep in Mind: Gamingfocused apps can be fantastic for finding someone who is just as passionate about games as you are, but keep an open mind about other interests too. Sometimes, finding someone who balances your love of gaming with a passion for something else can add a new spark to your life.

Gaming Tip: Do not just list every game you play; mention a few of your favorites and why you love them. This helps others get a feel for who you are and invites conversations that go beyond surface level.

2. For Book Lovers and Creative Types: Alikewise and Tastebuds

If you are a bookworm, love deep conversations, or are passionate about the arts, you know that shared interests can make all the difference. Apps like Alikewise and Tastebuds were created for people who bond over what they read, listen to, and watch. Alikewise focuses on books, matching people based on their favorite reads, while Tastebuds pairs people up based on music taste.

· Why It Works: When you connect with someone over a favorite book, album, or genre, it feels instantly personal. You are sharing a piece of yourself, not just a hobby. Platforms like these allow you to build your profile around what really moves you—whether it is that scifi series, you cannot stop reading or the playlist that gets you through your workday.

- Who It is For: This is ideal for people who believe that shared cultural interests say something meaningful about a person. If you love spending hours discussing books, films, or music and you are looking for someone who feels the same way, these platforms let you find people who already share those passions.
- Things to Keep in Mind: It is great to bond over mutual interests, but remember that interests can evolve. If you are interested in finding someone with a shared love of a specific book or band, that is a good start, but staying open to new things can keep the connection fresh.

Book/Music Tip: Instead of listing popular books or artists, pick a few that mean the most to you. These unique choices help spark conversations and make you stand out as someone who knows what they love.

3. For Nature Enthusiasts and the Outdoorsy: MeetMindful and Huggle

If you are someone who feels most alive when you are outdoors, in nature, or pursuing a lifestyle centered on mindfulness and wellness, there are platforms designed just for you. Apps like MeetMindful and Huggle cater to people who prioritize healthy living, selfcare, and an appreciation for nature.

- Why It Works: These platforms connect people with similar values around mindfulness, health, and wellness. MeetMindful allows users to connect over shared values and lifestyle choices, such as meditation, yoga, or ecoconscious living. Huggle, on the other hand, matches people based on shared places they have been, like favorite hiking spots or local parks.

- Who It is For: This is perfect if you are someone who loves activities like hiking, yoga, or even just long walks in nature. If your idea of a great date involves a nature trail instead of a movie theater or you would rather connect over shared values than shared media, these platforms can help you find people who get it.
- Things to Keep in Mind: MeetMindful and Huggle tend to attract people with a holistic approach to dating so that it can feel like a slower, more intentional experience. If you are serious about finding someone who shares these values, this can be an incredibly fulfilling way to meet new people.

Outdoor Tip: Share your favorite outdoor spots or mindful practices. This gives others a glimpse into your lifestyle and makes it easy to plan a date that feels authentic to both of you.

4. For the Culturally Connected: Shaadi and Aisle

For people who prioritize cultural connections and may be seeking a partner with shared values or family backgrounds, Shaadi and Aisle are popular choices in India. These platforms blend modern dating with traditional cultural elements, allowing you to meet people who appreciate both contemporary and traditional values.

- Why It Works: Shaadi and Aisle cater to individuals who are open to dating and marriage but want to meet people with a similar cultural or family background. They bring in elements that honor Indian traditions, and they are built for people who are looking for something meaningful and longterm.

- Who It is For: If you are someone who values your heritage and wants to share that with a partner, these platforms are a natural fit. They attract people who appreciate cultural connection and may be interested in dating with a view toward marriage.
- Things to Keep in Mind: These platforms tend to be focused on people who are looking for something serious, so if that is your intention, they could be a great fit. However, be prepared for a more indepth setup process, as the profiles are designed to capture values and family background.

Cultural Tip: Be open about your values and what you are looking for in a partner. This will help you attract people who share those values and create a solid foundation for future conversations.

Why Niche Platforms Can Make a Big Difference

Niche dating apps give you a chance to start with common ground, and that can make all the difference. Instead of worrying about whether your interests are 'too specific' or feeling like you have to explain your passions, these platforms bring people together who already understand each other on some level. It is about finding connections where there's already an understanding, where your quirks are seen as strengths, and your interests as conversation starters.

Staying Safe and Private Online

Let's be honest—online dating can be a mix of excitement and caution. With so many people out there, it is normal to feel a bit protective over your personal info. Online dating should feel comfortable, even fun, and a big part of that is knowing how to stay safe and keep your privacy intact while exploring new connections. Like meeting someone at a party or event, it is about pacing yourself and ensuring you are in control of what you share.

Here are some straightforward tips to help you stay secure and confident as you navigate online dating. Think of these as tools to help you enjoy the experience without stressing over every interaction.

1. Be Selective About What You Share.

When you are getting to know someone online, it is tempting to dive into a full 'about me' rundown, especially if the conversation is flowing. But in the early stages, it is smart to keep certain details to yourself.

- Stick to General Info First: Sharing that you love coffee or are into Marvel movies is great, but hold back on personal details like your exact address, where you work, or any specifics that make it easy for someone to track you down IRL. This way, you are staying open without revealing too much too soon.
- Use the App's Messaging System: Most dating apps have builtin messaging for a reason – it keeps your phone number and personal contacts private until you are

ready to share. Staying within the app also gives you the control to block or unmatch if things take an uncomfortable turn.

- Think Twice Before Sharing Social Media Links: Linking your Instagram or other social media profiles to your dating profile is optional. If you are not sure, it is perfectly fine to wait until you feel more comfortable with someone before giving them access to your social life.

Quick Tip: Remember, a first conversation online is a lot like meeting a stranger at a friend's party. You would not start with your life story right away, so take things one step at a time.

2. Get to Know the Privacy Settings.

Each dating platform has its own privacy settings, and taking a few minutes to understand them can give you a lot of control over who can reach you or see your profile.

- Adjust Profile Visibility: Many apps let you limit who can view your profile or message you. Some even let you stay hidden unless you have 'liked' someone first. These settings can help you filter out unwanted interactions, making the app experience smoother and more secure.
- Be Thoughtful with Photos: Choose photos that show who you are but do not reveal too much about your everyday life. Avoid shots that make it easy to figure out your routine or location, like a photo outside your favorite café or in front of your house.

- Understand Blocking and Reporting Options: Most apps allow you to block or report users who make you uncomfortable. Do not hesitate to use these tools if needed—they are there to keep the platform safe, and trusting your instincts is always a good idea.

Privacy Tip: Spend a few minutes exploring the privacy settings when you sign up for a new platform. A little knowledge upfront can help you feel more secure as you start connecting with people.

3. Watch for Red Flags

Like in real life social situations, trust your gut and stay alert for suspicious behaviors. While most people on dating apps are there for genuine reasons, it is always smart to look for signs that something is not right.

- Do not Share Financial Information: This might seem obvious, but it is worth repeating—never share financial information or give money to anyone you have just met online. Scammers sometimes ask for financial help, and any request for money is a major red flag.
- Be Cautious with Fast Intimacy: If someone you just met starts getting overly intense or pushing for a serious commitment quickly, it is usually a warning sign. Building trust takes time, and rushing the process can be a way to manipulate emotions. Take things at your own pace.
- Notice Inconsistencies: Pay attention to the details. If someone's stories do not add up or are evasive about basic questions, they may not be as genuine as they

appear. Authentic connections do not require constant explanation, so trust your instincts.

Red Flag Tip: If something feels off, it is better to be cautious than to ignore it. Your instincts are there for a reason—listen to them.

4. Look After Your Mental WellBeing

Online dating is fun, but it can get overwhelming if you are not careful. Remember, taking care of your mental wellbeing is just as important as protecting your physical safety.

- Set Boundaries for Time and Energy: If you find social interactions draining, be intentional about your time on dating apps. Endless swiping can lead to burnout, so give yourself permission to take breaks and respond only when you feel ready.
- Do not Take Rejections Personally: Rejection is a part of dating, but it is never easy. Remember, everyone has different preferences, and a mismatch does not define your worth. Stay focused on finding someone who appreciates you for who you are.
- Take Breaks When You Need Them: If online dating starts feeling overwhelming, it is okay to step back. Taking a breather can help you recharge and return with fresh energy. Approaching dating with balance makes the experience more enjoyable and less stressful.

Mental WellBeing Tip: Online dating should complement your life, not become the center of it. Make time for your hobbies, friends, and other interests to keep things in perspective.

Staying safe online does not have to be complicated. It is about following a few basic guidelines, trusting your instincts, and protecting yourself as you meet new people. These tips are here to help you enjoy the process, explore new connections, and focus on finding genuine interactions—while staying in control of your privacy and safety.

VIII

Transitioning from Online to Offline – Taking the Leap

Preparing for the First Meeting

You have been chatting, things are going well, and now it is time to take that next big step: meeting in person. This can be exciting and nervewracking all at once, and that is totally normal. The first meeting is your chance to see if the connection you have felt online translates into real life. It is where the chats, shared interests, and little jokes finally come facetoface.

Let's talk about a few things you can do to prepare, relax, and set yourself up for a great experience. This is not about trying to be someone you are not—it is about showing up as your real self, ready to enjoy the moment.

1. Choose a Comfortable, Public Place.

For a first meeting, it is best to keep things simple and choose a spot that feels comfortable. The idea is to meet somewhere that lets you have a conversation and feel at ease.

- Pick a Familiar Spot if You Can: If there's a café, a park, or a public place you enjoy, that is a great choice. Being somewhere familiar can help you feel grounded and give you a bit more confidence. Plus, if it is a place you genuinely like, you will naturally feel more at ease.
- Stay Public and Safe: Meeting in a public place, especially for the first time, is always a good idea. It keeps things casual and also adds a layer of safety. A café, a cozy brunch spot, or a lively but relaxed restaurant are ideal options because they let you focus on getting to know each other without too much pressure.
- Keep It Simple: There's no need to go overboard with a fancy or elaborate plan. A casual setting gives you both the freedom to leave after a quick coffee if things are not clicking—or extend the meeting if you are enjoying yourselves.

Tip: Choose a place where you can talk easily without too much noise or distraction. If you are not sure, pick somewhere with a relaxed vibe where the focus can be on your conversation.

2. Dress Comfortably and Be Yourself.

When it comes to dressing for the first date, the key is to look like yourself. Wear something that makes you feel confident but comfortable so you will not have to adjust your clothes or feel out of place. This is not about impressing them with a big fashion statement—it is about being true to who you are.

- Choose an Outfit That Feels Like 'You': Think about what you would wear to meet a friend in the same setting. Your outfit should reflect your personality while keeping you comfortable. If you are someone who loves a casual look, go with that. If you enjoy dressing up a bit, feel free to do so—just stay true to your style.
- Dress for the Setting: If you are meeting at a park, dress casually. If it is a café or a quiet restaurant, go for something neat but relaxed. Dressing for the place you are going will help you feel more comfortable and confident when you arrive.
- Do not Overthink It: It is easy to get caught up in trying to find the 'perfect' outfit, but remember, they are meeting you for who you are, not what you are wearing. Choose something that makes you feel good, and then focus on enjoying the moment.

Tip: If you are comfortable, you will come across as relaxed and approachable. Confidence shines through when you are genuinely feeling like yourself.

3. Have a Few Conversation Starters Ready.

Even if the conversation has been flowing smoothly online, it is natural to feel a bit nervous in person. Having a few topics or questions in mind can be a great way to break the ice and keep things moving if there's a lull.

- Bring Up Something You have Talked About Online: Reference something you have discussed in your chats—maybe it is a shared interest, a funny story, or a favorite book or movie you have discussed. This not only makes the conversation feel familiar but also shows that you remember and care about what they shared.
- Ask OpenEnded Questions: Keep it light and open. Questions like "What's something interesting you've done recently?" or "If you could travel anywhere right now, where would you go?" give them a chance to share more about themselves without feeling put on the spot.
- Share a Bit About Yourself: Conversations are not just about questions. Feel free to share something about your day, a funny incident, or a recent experience. Sharing a bit about yourself balances the conversation and helps your date get to know you too.

Tip: It is okay to have some 'starter' topics in mind, but do not feel like you need to script the conversation. Just be yourself and let things unfold naturally.

4. Keep Your Expectations Low and Your Mind Open

This is the first time you are meeting in person, so give yourself and your date the freedom to see where things go. It is normal to feel hopeful, but keeping your expectations realistic can make the experience more enjoyable.

- Do not Expect Magic Right Away: Sometimes, a great connection takes a little time to develop in person. Chemistry online does not always translate immediately in real life, and that is okay. Be open to the experience without expecting everything to fall perfectly into place immediately.

- Stay in the Moment: It is easy to start analyzing everything but try to stay present. Enjoy the moment and focus on having a good time rather than overthinking what each little gesture or comment might mean.

- Remember, It is Just One Meeting: This first meeting is not about deciding your future together. It is just a chance to get to know each other better. If things go well, great! And if not, that is okay too. You have taken a step, and each experience brings you closer to finding the right match.

Tip: Take a few deep breaths before you meet. Remind yourself that this is just one part of the journey and enjoy the process.

5. Plan for an Easy Exit (Just in Case)

First dates are all about discovery, and sometimes things do not go as expected. It is perfectly okay to keep things short if you are not feeling a connection.

- Set a Time Limit: If you are unsure, set a timeframe for the date—say, an hour for coffee. That way, if it is going well, you can always extend it. And if it is not, you have a natural ending point that does not feel awkward.

- Let a Friend Know Your Plans: Share your meeting location and a rough timeline with a friend. This is not only a good safety measure, but it also gives you the option to have someone to chat with afterwards, whether things went well or not.
- Trust Your Gut: If something does not feel right, it is okay to call it a day. You do not owe anyone a long explanation or extended time if it does not feel comfortable. Thank them for the meetup and make your exit gracefully.

Tip: Knowing you have an easy exit plan can actually make you feel more relaxed. You are in control and free to leave if you need to.

Meeting someone for the first time in person can feel like a big step, but remember, it is just one part of your journey. Stay true to yourself, keep things light, and let the experience unfold naturally. You have put in the effort to get to know each other online, and now it is time to take that next step with confidence and a positive outlook.

Reading Body Language and Chemistry

So, you have made it to the first in person meeting! Now, you are probably wondering how to figure out if there's a genuine spark or connection. While words can tell us a lot, body language and subtle cues often reveal even more. Reading body language and chemistry is not about analyzing every little move; it is about being present and noticing how you feel around each other.

Let's walk through some practical ways to pick up on these signals so you can get a clearer sense of the vibe and enjoy the experience without secondguessing everything.

1. Start by Observing the Basics: Smiles, Eye Contact, and Posture

One of the easiest ways to gauge someone's interest and comfort is by noticing their basic body language. Simple cues like smiles, eye contact, and open posture can give you a sense of how they feel in the moment.

- Genuine Smiles Mean a Lot: A real, relaxed smile can say more than words. If they are smiling often and it looks genuine—think of a smile that reaches the eyes—that is usually a good sign that they enjoy themselves and feel comfortable around you.
- Eye Contact Shows Interest: Making eye contact is a classic way to show interest and build a connection. If they are holding eye contact with you (without it feeling forced or intense), it is a positive sign. If they look away occasionally or seem a bit shy, that is okay too; it might just mean they are a bit nervous, which is normal.
- Look for an Open, Relaxed Posture: How someone sits or stands can give you a sense of their comfort level. If they are facing you with an open posture—meaning no crossed arms, leaning slightly toward you, or mirroring your movements—it often indicates they are engaged and at ease. Crossed arms or turning away might mean they are a little guarded, but it could also just be a sign of nerves.

Tip: Try not to overanalyze. A natural smile or a relaxed posture is a good sign, but if they seem a little stiff at first, give them (and yourself) time to settle in.

2. Notice Signs of Chemistry Without Forcing It

Chemistry can seem mysterious, but often, it is about shared energy and comfort in each other's company. The trick is to notice these moments without putting pressure on yourself—or them—to make something happen.

- Do You Both Lean In? If you are both naturally leaning in toward each other, it is a subtle sign of interest. People who feel a connection tend to close the physical distance a bit. If you find yourself mirroring each other's posture—like crossing your arms or resting your hands in similar ways—it is often a sign that you are connecting on a deeper level.
- Are There Comfortable Pauses? Chemistry does not mean talking nonstop. Sometimes, a comfortable silence or a shared laugh without words says a lot. If you can be quiet together without feeling awkward, it is often a sign of a natural connection. These pauses let you enjoy each other's presence without needing to fill every second with conversation.
- Look for Playfulness or Light Touches: If they are feeling comfortable, they might initiate small, natural touches—like a tap on the arm during a laugh or brushing a piece of lint off your shoulder. Light, friendly touches (if they feel natural and welcome) often signal interest and comfort. If physical touch is not their thing,

that is fine too; people show interest in different ways.

Tip: Chemistry does not always mean instant fireworks. Sometimes, it is a quieter sense of ease. Do not rush to label the feeling—just enjoy being in the moment and see how it unfolds.

3. Checkin with How You are Feeling, Too

Reading body language is not just about the other person. How you feel around them matters just as much. If you are noticing a sense of comfort or excitement, that is just as valuable as any nonverbal cues.

- Are You Feeling Relaxed? Notice your own body language and feelings. Are you able to sit comfortably, make eye contact, and feel at ease? If you find yourself genuinely laughing, smiling, and relaxing, that is a good sign that you are connecting in a real way.
- Do You Feel 'Seen'? A great first meeting often involves feeling truly 'seen' by the other person. If they are listening, engaging with your stories, and making you feel heard, it is likely that there's a connection forming. Chemistry often comes down to feeling understood and appreciated.
- Is the Energy Balanced? Ideally, you will both be contributing equally to the conversation. If it feels like you are carrying the conversation or if they are talking without giving you space, that is worth noticing. Good chemistry often feels balanced, with each person showing genuine interest in the other.

Tip: Trust your gut. If you are feeling good, relaxed, and genuinely happy in their company, there's a good chance the chemistry is mutual.

4. Stay Open and Do not Overthink It

Body language and chemistry are useful clues, but do not feel pressured to make a decision based on the first impression alone. Sometimes, chemistry builds over time as you get to know each other better.

- Keep an Open Mind: If you are not feeling immediate sparks, that does not necessarily mean the connection will not grow. Some of the best relationships start slowly, with comfort and compatibility developing over time. Give yourself permission to enjoy the moment without stressing over what it 'should' feel like.
- Remember That People Show Interest Differently: Not everyone expresses interest in the same way. Some people are naturally more reserved or may need a bit more time to open up. Give each other space to be yourselves and do not rush to judge based on one interaction.
- Focus on Enjoying Yourself: The best first meetings are the ones where you can have fun, share a few laughs, and get a genuine feel for each other's personalities. If you are having a good time, let that be enough for now. There's plenty of time to see where things go.

Tip: Treat the first meeting as just that—a meeting. There's no need to label it as anything more. Enjoy getting to know someone new, and let the rest unfold naturally.

The first meeting is an exciting step, but it is just one part of the journey. Body language and chemistry are helpful indicators, but they are not the whole story. Stay present, keep an open mind, and let yourself enjoy the experience without putting too much pressure on what it 'should' feel like. Often, the best connections are the ones that happen when you are relaxed and just being yourself.

Deciding on Next Steps

So, you have met in person, shared a few laughs, and hopefully enjoyed each other's company. Now what? This is the time to think about where you'd like things to go and how to handle that allimportant "What's next?" without feeling stressed or pressured.

Let's review some simple ways to reflect on how things went, clarify your intentions, and decide what comes next, whether that means planning a second meetup or gently parting ways. Remember, this process is not about overthinking or trying to get it all right. It is just about being honest with yourself and with them as you take the next step in your journey.

1. Take a Moment to Reflect on How You Felt

After the first meeting, it is natural to feel a mix of emotions—maybe excitement, curiosity, or even some uncertainty. Taking a little time to reflect on the experience can help you get clear about whether you are interested in seeing them again or if it might be best to move on.

- Ask Yourself How You Felt Overall: Think back on the vibe of the date. Did you feel comfortable? Did the conversation flow naturally? If you feel relaxed and at ease, that is usually a good sign. If there are awkward moments, do not stress too much; sometimes, people need a little time to warm up. But if something felt truly off, it is worth considering if you want to continue.
- Notice Your Energy Levels: A good first date often leaves you feeling energized, curious, or even excited to learn more about them. If you left the date feeling drained, frustrated, or uneasy, that is something to pay attention to. Trust your gut—your natural reaction to the experience can often tell you what you need to know.
- Reflect on What You Enjoyed Most: Was there something specific that made you enjoy the date? Maybe you connected over a shared interest, laughed at the same jokes or had a genuinely good conversation. Pinpointing these moments can help you decide if it is worth exploring the connection further.

Reflection Tip: Do not overthink it. Go with your honest feelings. If you feel good about the date and want to see where it goes, that is enough reason to give it another chance.

2. Be Honest with Yourself About What You are Looking For

After you have had a chance to reflect, it is time to ask yourself what you really want from this connection. Are you open to seeing where things go, or are you looking for something specific, like a serious relationship or a casual friendship? Knowing your intentions can help you decide on your next move.

- Think About What Feels Right for You Right Now: Your goals might be different from theirs, and that is okay. If you are looking for something serious, pay attention to whether this person seems like they might be on the same page. If you are just interested in meeting new people and seeing what happens, that is fine too—just be clear with yourself about what you want.
- Consider How They Made You Feel: Did they make you feel respected, heard, and appreciated? A good connection, even in its early stages, should feel positive and supportive. If you are questioning their intentions or feel uncomfortable, it might be worth taking a step back.
- Decide If You are Excited About a Second Meeting: Ask yourself if you genuinely would like to meet them again. If the answer is yes, go for it! If you are unsure or feel hesitant, listen to that feeling. It is better to take things slow than to rush into something that does not feel right.

Clarity Tip: There's no right or wrong answer here. Go with what feels best for you at this moment, and do not feel pressured to have everything figured out.

3. Communicate Openly About Next Steps

When you are ready to decide on what comes next, open and honest communication can make things a lot smoother. Whether you are excited about another date or feeling uncertain, sharing your thoughts openly (but kindly) helps set the tone for what is to come.

- If You are Interested, Keep It Simple: If you enjoyed the first meeting and want to meetup again, there's no need to play games or hold back. A simple "I had a great time and would love to do this again if you are interested" lets them know you are open to a second date without any pressure.
- If You are Unsure, Take Your Time: If you are feeling on the fence, that is completely okay. Sometimes, it takes a little more time to know if there's a real connection. If they reach out, you could suggest another casual meetup and see how it goes, or be honest about needing more time. It is all about doing what feels right for you.
- If It is Not a Match, Be Respectful: If you have decided it is not a fit, it is best to let them know politely. A simple message like, "Thanks for meeting up—it was great to get to know you. I am not sure we are a match, but I enjoyed our time together," is kind and clear. Most people appreciate honesty, and this allows you both to move forward respectfully.

Communication Tip: When in doubt, honesty is the best approach. Clear communication helps avoid misunderstandings and sets a positive tone, whether you are planning another date or choosing to move on.

4. Make Plans for a Second Date (If You are Both Interested)

If things went well and you are both interested in seeing each other again, do not overthink the second date. Keep it casual and choose something that feels relaxed, so you can both continue getting to know each other without too much pressure.

- Choose a LowKey Activity: The second date does not need to be a big event. A coffee date, a casual lunch, or a walk in a park are great options. The goal is just to spend more time together in a comfortable setting.
- Try Something That Allows for Conversation: Opt for an activity where you can talk, like visiting a local market, checking out a museum, or grabbing ice cream. This way, you will get to interact in a relaxed setting, making it easier to see if the connection is there.
- Stay Open to the Flow: Just like the first date, the second is about enjoying the experience. There's no need to rush into anything or set specific expectations. The best connections often develop naturally when both people are relaxed and enjoying each other's company.

Second Date Tip: Make it fun and light. The goal is to keep getting to know each other and see where things go.

5. Learn from each date and enjoy the journey!

Whether the first date was amazing, just okay, or not a match, try not to dwell too much on the outcome. Each experience brings you one step closer to understanding what you want and who is right for you. Do not be like Rajesh from 'The Big Bang Theory' who tends to overthink every step when he dates!

- Enjoy the Journey: Dating is a journey, and every experience is valuable in its own way. If this connection did not work out, it is simply part of the process. And if it did go well, great—you have taken a step forward and can enjoy seeing where it leads.

- Celebrate Your Effort: Meeting someone new and putting yourself out there takes courage, and that is worth recognizing. Every date is a chance to learn more about yourself and grow. Take pride in the fact that you are investing in your happiness.
- Keep an Open Mind Moving Forward: The next steps do not have to be clearcut. Take it one step at a time, and trust that each meeting, conversation, and connection brings you closer to finding the right match.

Perspective Tip: Remind yourself that this is just one part of your journey. Enjoy the process, stay open, and trust that the right connection is out there.

Deciding on the next steps is all about trusting yourself and being honest with what feels right. Whether it leads to a second date, a friendship, or simply a great story to look back on, each experience brings value. Stay true to yourself, communicate openly, and remember—you are building a journey that is unique to you.

IX

Building and Sustaining an Interesting Relationship

Keeping Communication Consistent

So you have hit it off, and now you are wondering how to keep that spark alive. The truth is, in any relationship, communication is what keeps things grounded. Whether you are an introvert, a geek, a mix of both, or something else entirely, keeping the lines open and the conversation flowing can make all the difference in growing a connection that lasts. But consistency does not mean you have to talk 24/7 or put on a 'perfect' face all the time. It is more about finding a rhythm that works for both of you and staying real along the way.

Here are some tips for keeping communication steady, meaningful, and genuine as you build your relationship.

1. Find Your Own Natural Flow

Not everyone has the same communication style, and that is completely okay. Some people like to check in often, while others are content with a few quality conversations throughout the week. The goal is to figure out what feels right for both of you and make it work without forcing anything.

- Get a Sense of Each Other's Preferences: Some people are natural texters, while others prefer phone calls or even the occasional video chat. Ask your partner what feels most natural for them and share what works best for you, too. This helps set a comfortable pace and avoids misunderstandings.
- Start Small, Then Build from There: In the beginning, keeping things light and fun is often the best approach. A simple "How is your day going?" or sharing something interesting you saw or read can go a long way. Over time, you will naturally find the balance between daily check ins and more indepth conversations.
- Avoid 'Overthinking' Communication Frequency: It is easy to fall into the trap of wondering if you are texting too much or too little. Instead, focus on quality. If you both enjoy a few quick check ins and a deeper chat here and there, let that be your rhythm. The best flow is one that feels effortless and keeps you both engaged without the pressure.

Tip: If you are both comfortable, consider setting up a casual routine, like an endofday check in or a weekend call. It keeps things consistent but relaxed.

2. Balance Talking and Listening

Great communication is not just about talking—it is also about listening. One of the best ways to build a strong connection is by genuinely listening to each other's thoughts, ideas, and even the little details that make up everyday life.

- Give Them Room to Share: When you ask how their day went or what is on their mind, make sure to give them space to actually open up. Sometimes, just listening without jumping in with advice or your own stories makes the other person feel heard and appreciated.
- Show Interest in Their Passions: If they are into something you do not know much about—whether it is a hobby, a favorite show, or a skill—ask questions and show genuine interest. People enjoy sharing what they are passionate about, and your interest shows that you care about the things that make them unique.
- Share Your Own Stories and Perspectives:
- Listening is crucial, but sharing your own experiences keeps the conversation balanced. Do not worry about trying to be impressive or 'deep'—just be yourself. Share things that genuinely interest you or moments from your day. This backandforth keeps things engaging and allows both of you to feel understood.

Listening Tip: Take mental notes of things they mention—like an upcoming project, a favorite band, or something they are excited about. Following up on these details later shows you are paying attention and adds a personal touch to your communication.

3. Be Honest About Your Feelings and Needs

When it comes to building a lasting connection, honesty is your best friend. It is easy to go along with things in the early stages, trying to keep things smooth, but true closeness comes from being upfront about what you need and how you feel.

- Share What You Need to Feel Connected: If you are someone who values regular communication, let them know. Or, if you need more space to recharge (something many introverts relate to), it is okay to communicate that too. Letting them know upfront helps create a dynamic where both people's needs are respected.
- Be Open with Your Emotions: It is natural to have good days and off days, and you do not need to pretend otherwise. If you are feeling stressed or had a rough day, sharing that honestly (without venting too heavily) can actually bring you closer. Being open about both the highs and lows creates a more genuine connection.
- Address Misunderstandings Early: If something feels off, do not hesitate to talk about it in a straightforward but kind way. Maybe there was a missed text or an offhand comment that did not sit right. Clearing up small things early on helps avoid larger misunderstandings later.

Honesty Tip: It is okay to keep it simple, honesty does not have to be a heavy conversation. Just a quick, "Hey, this is how I feel about this" can go a long way.

4. Keep It Fun and Playful

Consistency does not mean all serious conversations. Keeping things fun and lighthearted helps build a relationship where both of you feel free to be yourselves. Small, playful moments can make communication feel natural and enjoyable, keeping things from feeling like a chore.

- Share Little Everyday Moments: Snap a photo of your morning coffee, share a funny meme, or tell them about something silly that happened in your day. These small, everyday shares add personality to your conversations and let you stay connected even when life is busy.
- Create Inside Jokes or Shared Hobbies: If you discover something you both enjoy—whether it is a show, a game, or even a weird internet meme—keep that going. Inside jokes and shared interests give your conversations an added layer of familiarity and fun.
- Surprise Them with Something Unexpected: Whether it is a random compliment, a funny memory, or something you noticed they like, small surprises keep communication fresh. A quick "I thought of you when I saw this" can brighten their day and make them feel special.

Fun Tip: Do not be afraid to mix things up. Send a random joke, suggest a quick video call, or plan a virtual 'game night' if you are in a longdistance setup. Playfulness keeps things interesting and keeps you both looking forward to the next conversation.

5. Know When to Step Back and Recharge

Even in a relationship, it is essential to take time for yourself. Staying connected is important, but so is recharging, especially for introverts who need that downtime. It is all about finding a balance where both of you feel connected without burning out.

- Communicate When You Need Some Space: If you are feeling drained and need a little time to yourself, let them know. A simple message like, "I'm taking a quiet night tonight, looking forward to catching up tomorrow!" is usually more than enough. They will appreciate your honesty, and it keeps things balanced.
- Respect Their Need for Space Too: Relationships are all about respecting each other's boundaries. If they need some time for themselves or have a busy week, do not take it personally. Allowing each other the space to recharge helps keep things healthy and sustainable.
- Reconnect When You are Ready: After some time to yourself, reconnect with something meaningful, like a story from your day or a funny moment you wanted to share. This way, you show them that even though you needed space, they are still on your mind.

Recharge Tip: Taking time to recharge makes your connection stronger in the long run. A little space every now and then helps you both come back to the relationship with fresh energy and a clearer head.

Keeping communication consistent is all about finding a natural flow that feels good for both of you. It does not have to be perfect or intense – it is more about staying genuine, showing up in small ways, and giving each other the freedom to connect at your own pace.

Creating Shared Experiences and Memories

When it comes to building a connection that lasts, shared experiences and memories are key. Think of them as the little anchors that keep you grounded together, even when life gets busy or routine. Making time for memorable moments does not mean grand gestures or perfectly planned dates. It is about finding joy in everyday experiences, creating traditions, and building moments that are just for the two of you.

Let's dive into some simple, meaningful ways to create these memories and experiences—things that can keep the relationship fresh, fun, and uniquely yours.

1. Celebrate the Little Moments Together

Special memories do not have to come from big events. Sometimes, the smallest moments end up meaning the most. By making a habit of celebrating the little things, you are creating a relationship filled with joy and positivity, no matter what the day holds.

- Celebrate Each Other's Wins, Big or Small: Did they complete a work project, hit a personal goal, or finally finish that book they have been reading? Acknowledge it! Even a simple "I am proud of you" or a toast over dinner can turn an ordinary day into something memorable. It is these little celebrations that make everyday life feel a bit more special.

- Make Ordinary Moments Fun: Some of the best memories come from unexpected, spontaneous fun. Turn a grocery run into an adventure by picking out a random new snack to try together. Or make cleaning day more enjoyable by playing music and dancing around the room. Sometimes, it is the silly, unplanned moments that stick with you the most.

- Start Simple Traditions: Traditions do not have to be tied to the holidays. Something as simple as a Friday night movie ritual or making pancakes together on Sundays can become a cherished part of your relationship. These routines give you both something to look forward to and create shared experiences that become uniquely yours.

Celebration Tip: Snap a quick photo or make a small note of these moments. Over time, they will add up to a collection of memories you can look back on together.

2. Explore New Activities and Hobbies Together

One of the best ways to keep things interesting is by stepping out of your comfort zone together. Exploring new activities or hobbies adds variety, keeps the relationship fresh, and helps you both grow as individuals and as a couple.

- Try Something Neither of You Has Done Before: Whether it is taking a cooking class, going on a hike, or trying out a new sport, learning something new together brings a sense of adventure. Plus, it creates an experience that is unique to both of you. Even if you are not great at it, you will both have fun figuring it out and making memories in the process.
- Share Each Other's Interests: If one of you has a hobby the other does not know much about, try inviting them into it. Maybe you are into gaming, or they love painting. Spend an afternoon together learning about each other's passions, even if it is just for fun. It is a great way to show that you care about what makes them tick.
- Go on 'MiniAdventures': Not every adventure has to be a vacation. Exploring a new café, taking a scenic drive, or checking out a local event can feel like an adventure without the big commitment. These mini outings add variety to your time together, creating memories beyond the usual dinner dates.

Adventure Tip: Keep a 'bucket list' of things you would like to try together. This will give you a steady source of ideas for spontaneous plans and keep things exciting over time.

3. Build Connection Through Shared Interests and Inside Jokes

Shared interests often bring two people together, but shared jokes, references, and memories make a relationship feel like it is 'yours'. Building up these little connections creates a sense of familiarity and deepens your bond in a way that feels natural and unique.

- Create Your Own Inside Jokes: If you find yourselves laughing over a shared joke or a silly moment, keep it going! Inside jokes make you feel connected like you are in on a little secret only the two of you share. Whether it is a goofy nickname or a joke about that one time you got lost on the way to a restaurant, these little things bring you closer.
- Discover 'Your Thing': Couples often have 'their thing'—a favorite show, a mutual love for a certain band, or a shared hobby. If there's something you both enjoy, embrace it! Having something you both love gives you a goto activity that is always fun and familiar, whether it is a series you bingewatch together or a board game you both cannot get enough of.
- Revisit Memorable Moments Regularly: A big part of sustaining a relationship is reflecting on the good times you have shared. Reminisce about a funny experience, look back at old photos together, or share what you love most about past dates. Revisiting these memories strengthens the bond and reminds you both of all the good things you have together.

Connection Tip: Start a 'Memory Jar' where you jot down fun memories or quotes from your time together. Over time, you will have a whole collection of moments to look back on.

4. Keep the Spark Alive with Surprises and Thoughtful Gestures

Consistency is important, but so is the occasional surprise. Small gestures and spontaneous acts of kindness show you are thinking about each other, adding that extra layer of excitement and thoughtfulness to the relationship.

- Surprise Them with Something Simple: A surprise does not need to be extravagant. Sending them a quick "thinking of you" message, leaving a note in their bag, or bringing them their favorite snack can brighten their day and show you are paying attention to the little things.
- Plan a Surprise Date or Activity: Every so often, plan something a little different— a movie night with their favorite film, a spontaneous road trip, or even a picnic in the park. Surprises keep things fresh and remind them that you are still as invested in creating new experiences together as you were at the start.
- Celebrate 'Just Because' Moments: Who says you need an occasion to do something special? Celebrate random days just because. Make breakfast in bed, plan a fun game night, or do something you know they love, purely to make them smile. These little gestures can mean even more than big events because they show thoughtfulness and care in everyday life.

Surprise Tip: Keep a few small 'surprise ideas' in mind for those days when you want to do soumething extra. It does not have to be fancy—sometimes, a thoughtful note or a favorite treat says it all. Creating shared experiences and memories is not about grand gestures or meticulously planned dates. It is about finding joy in the ordinary, embracing new adventures together, and building up a collection of moments that belong just to you. Every memory, inside joke, and small tradition strengthens your connection, keeping the relationship interesting, meaningful, and full of life.

Handling Conflicts and LongDistance Dynamics

Let's face it: every relationship has its fair share of ups and downs, and the closer we get to someone, the more likely we are to bump into a few disagreements or obstacles. Whether it is a minor squabble or the challenge of managing longdistance love, handling these moments with patience and honesty can make all the difference. Think of it as approaching each bump in the road as a team—you are in this together, and every challenge is just another chance to grow stronger.

Here are some practical, lowkey ways to navigate conflicts and keep that connection strong, even when you are miles apart.

1. Approach Conflict as a Team

Conflicts do not have to feel like battles; they can be opportunities to understand each other better. The trick? Treat every disagreement as "us vs. the issue" instead of "me vs. you." When you view conflicts as something to tackle together, you are setting the stage for constructive solutions rather than letting things get tense or personal.

- Keep Communication Calm and Respectful: When something's bothering you, start the conversation calmly. Instead of diving straight in, you might begin with, "There's something I have been wanting to talk about—are you open to it?" Keeping your tone easygoing invites open dialogue and can help both of you feel at ease.
- Listen to Understand, Not Just to Reply: It is easy to get caught up in our own perspective, but genuinely listening to theirs can shift everything. Let them share without jumping in or assuming. You do not have to agree but listening shows respect and creates a space where you can work together on a solution.
- Focus on Solutions Over Blame: Skip the blame game and look forward. Instead of "Why did you do this?" try, "What can we both do to avoid this next time?" This approach reinforces that you are both committed to making things better, rather than dwelling on what went wrong.

Conflict Tip: Take a breather if things feel too heated. A quick pause can make a world of difference, helping you both return to the conversation with a clearer mind and calmer tone.

2. Build Trust and Stability in a LongDistance Relationship

Longdistance relationships come with their own unique challenges, but they also open up chances to grow closer in new ways. Building trust, creating routines, and finding creative ways to stay connected can help you both feel secure, even when you are separated by miles.

- Set Up a Regular Communication Routine: Having a set time to connect, whether it is a nightly call or a weekend video chat, can create a sense of stability. It does not have to be lengthy; even a quick check in can keep you both feeling close and connected.
- Be Open About Expectations and Boundaries: In longdistance relationships, clarity is your best friend. Be upfront about what you each need—whether it is around communication, visits, or social boundaries. Being on the same page helps avoid misunderstandings and creates a sense of mutual respect.
- Plan Visits When Possible: If possible, having visits on the calendar gives you both something to look forward to. Even if visits are not frequent, knowing there's a future date makes the distance feel more manageable.

LongDistance Tip: Use technology to bridge the gap. Whether it is voice messages, video calls, or surprise texts, these small gestures can make you feel closer, even on the longest days.

3. Keep the Connection Strong with Creativity and Thoughtfulness

Whether you are working through a disagreement or dealing with longdistance challenges, a bit of creativity can help you both feel connected and appreciated. Thoughtful gestures go a long way in reminding each other that you are committed to keeping the relationship alive and well.

- Send a Random "Thinking of You" Message: A spontaneous "thinking of you" text, a funny meme, or a quick voice note can make a big difference. These small reminders show that you are on each other's minds, even when life gets busy.
- Surprise Each Other with Simple Acts of Care: If you are longdistance, a care package or handwritten note is a great way to show you are thinking of them. If you're navigating a conflict, a thoughtful gesture—like sharing their favorite snack or leaving a quick note—can be a way to say, "We're still in this together."
- Create Small Rituals to Look Forward To: Rituals, even tiny ones, give you both something stable and positive. It could be a Friday night video call, a Zoom movie date, or both watching the same show and texting about it afterward. These small traditions create a sense of normalcy and give you both something to anticipate.

Creativity Tip: Keep a list of easy ideas for connecting, like sharing a photo of something that reminded you of them or planning a virtual 'date night'. These little moments keep things fresh and make the distance feel shorter.

4. Embrace Challenges as Opportunities to Grow

No relationship is perfect, and every bump in the road is a chance to learn and grow together. Whether it is handling a disagreement or dealing with the distance, each challenge can help you understand each other better and build a foundation of trust.

- Reflect on What You have Learned: After working through a challenge, take a moment to think about what you have learned. Maybe you discovered something about their perspective, or maybe you found a new way to communicate. Each experience, big or small, adds to the foundation of your relationship.
- Celebrate Small Wins: Getting through a tough spot or making it through a stretch of longdistance is worth acknowledging. Celebrating your efforts and commitment reminds you both of why you are in this together.
- See Each Other as a Team: When conflicts or distance feel like obstacles, remind yourselves that you are on the same side. You are both working toward a shared goal—building a strong, lasting connection. Embrace challenges as part of your journey, knowing they are adding layers to the story you are building together.

Growth Tip: After resolving a conflict or reuniting after time apart, plan something special to enjoy together. It could be a casual day out, a cozy night in, or even just a long, easy conversation. Reconnecting like this reinforces your bond and lets you appreciate each other's company even more.

Final Thoughts

Conflict and distance are just parts of any relationship journey. When you approach thm with respect, patience, and a team mindset, they can actually strengthen your bond. Remember, it is not about avoiding every challenge but about navigating them together, one honest conversation at a time. Keep communication open, focus on the big picture, and enjoy the journey of growing closer, no matter where life takes you.

X

Healing after heartbreak and Looking Ahead

SelfCare for Introverts

Breakups hurt. There's no sugarcoating it. For introverts, the process can feel even more overwhelming because we tend to process emotions deeply and privately. We replay conversations in our heads, analyze what went wrong, and sometimes retreat inward, carrying the weight of heartbreak alone. It is exhausting. But here is the thing: healing is possible, and it does not require you to change who you are. In fact, as an introvert, you already have tools within you to navigate this pain in a thoughtful, introspective way.

This chapter is not about moving on overnight—it is about equipping yourself with strategies rooted in selfcare, science, and compassion so you can embrace the healing process as the unique, introspective person you are.

1. Understand What is Happening in Your Brain and Body

Let's start with a little science. Breakups are painful because they affect your brain like physical pain. Studies have shown that the same areas of the brain that activate when you get physically injured also light up during heartbreak. So, if it feels like you are physically aching, you are not imagining it—your brain is literally processing the loss as pain.

For introverts, this can hit harder because we often spend a lot of time reflecting on the relationship, making the emotional pain more intense. That is not a bad thing; it just means we need to approach healing in a way that aligns with how we process emotions.

2. Create a Quiet Space to Grieve

Introverts recharge in solitude, and during a breakup, this can be a powerful tool. Carve out time and space to feel your emotions without judgment. This is not about wallowing – it is about allowing yourself to process the loss in a safe, quiet environment.

- Write it Out: Journaling is a proven method to process emotions and gain clarity. Set aside time each day to write down your feelings, no matter how messy they seem. Ask yourself questions like, "What am I feeling right now?" or "What did I learn from this relationship?"

- Name Your Emotions: Research shows that labeling emotions can help reduce their intensity. Instead of saying, "I'm overwhelmed," try, "I feel sadness, anger, and confusion." Naming these feelings gives you control over them, instead of letting them control you.

3. Lean Into SelfCompassion

Introverts often have a habit of overanalyzing and blaming themselves when things go wrong. But a breakup is not just one person's fault—it is the result of two people growing apart. Be kind to yourself during this process.

- Practice SelfTalk: Speak to yourself like you would to a friend. If your inner voice says, "I should have done better," counter it with, "I did the best I could with what I knew at the time."
- Forgive Yourself: Healing does not mean forgetting the relationship or the mistakes made along the way. It means acknowledging that you are human and giving yourself permission to let go of guilt and selfblame.

4. Reconnect With What Brings You Joy

Introverts often draw joy from meaningful activities—reading, creative projects, or exploring a quiet interest. Use this time to reconnect with the things that make you happy outside of the relationship. It is not about distraction; it is about rediscovering yourself.

- Start a Project: Whether it is learning something new, starting a small creative endeavor, or finally diving into that scifi series you have been meaning to watch, channeling your energy into a passion can be deeply fulfilling.

- Create Rituals: Simple routines, like a weekly movie night or a daily walk in nature, can provide comfort and stability. Rituals anchor you when everything else feels uncertain.

5. Build (and Lean on) a Support System

Even if you are someone who values solitude, it is important to reach out when you need it. Introverts thrive on deep, meaningful connections, so rely on the people you trust most—whether that is a close friend, a family member, or even a therapist.

- Choose Quality Over Quantity: You do not need to talk to everyone about your breakup. Pick one or two people who understand you and make you feel heard. Share as much or as little as you are comfortable with.
- Join a Community: If you are not ready to talk to someone in your personal life, consider joining an online group or forum for people going through breakups. Sometimes, connecting with strangers who understand your pain can be surprisingly healing.

6. Give Yourself Permission to Let Go

One of the hardest parts of a breakup is letting go of the 'whatifs'. For introverts, these thoughts can loop endlessly, keeping us stuck in a cycle of selfblame or longing. But letting go does not mean forgetting—it means accepting the reality of what was and making space for what is next.

- Create a 'Goodbye' Ritual: Write a letter to your ex (you do not have to send it) expressing everything you feel—good, bad, and in between. Then, destroy it in a way that feels symbolic to you. This act can help you create emotional closure.
- Focus on the Present: When you catch yourself drifting into the past, gently bring your focus back to the present moment. Meditation, breathing exercises, or even a simple grounding technique like naming five things you can see can help.

7. Set Small Goals for Moving Forward

Healing does not happen overnight, and that is okay. Instead of trying to 'get over it', focus on small, achievable goals. Each step forward is progress.

- Make One Small Change: Rearrange your living space, try a new hobby, or even switch up your daily routine. These small shifts remind you that life is still moving forward, and so are you.
- Celebrate Milestones: Whether it is going a day without crying or realizing you smiled for the first time in weeks, acknowledge these moments. Healing is a journey, and every step counts.

Embrace the Journey

Breakups are tough, but they are also a chance to grow, to rediscover yourself, and to create space for something new. As an introvert who has experience with a breakup or two, I am sure you have the ability to reflect deeply and find meaning in this process, even if it feels painful right now. Getting over somebody you loved will take time. Be patient with yourself, lean into your unique strengths, and remember—you are not just moving on. You are moving forward.

Take your time, trust yourself, and know that brighter days are ahead.

Finding Confidence in Being Yourself

Before anything else, here is something I want you to know being yourself is enough. If you take one lesson from this book, let it be this.

When you are genuinely you, you are opening the door to connections that are real and rewarding. For introverts, nerds, and geeks—especially those of us who may have tried to fit into boxes that were not made for us—finding confidence in our true selves is a journey. But the more we lean into who we really are, the more we'll connect with people who appreciate us just as we are.

This section is about embracing that journey. Confidence is not something you wake up with one day. It is built, step by step, by learning to value yourself and letting go of the need to prove anything.

As a child who grew up until he was seven years old in a small country in Latin America, moved to the Netherlands in Europe, and looks like someone living in India, I have had my share of experiences on how to connect two, actually three cultures in one mind. Conflict and uncertainty about who I was, am, and would like to be, have taken up a large part of my life. I have learned many lessons on how to behave as expected from my parents with family traditions as in India, my Western friends, and later in time, my colleagues.

With this background, I hope to give the tips below:

1. Recognize What Makes You, You—and Why That is a Good Thing

The world is full of people trying to fit into predefined categories or appear a certain way. But in reality, the qualities that make you stand out—the quirks, interests, and passions—are the ones that make you truly interesting. Recognizing your uniqueness is not just about selflove; it is about understanding what you bring to the table in a relationship.

- Value Your Passions and Hobbies: Whether you love Marvel movies, have an obsession with coding, or can lose yourself in hours of gaming, these are part of who you are. These interests are not just "things you like"—they are a window into what inspires and excites you. When you share these passions, you are offering a glimpse of your true self. The right person will find these qualities captivating and enjoy exploring them alongside you.

- See Your Introversion as a Strength: Introversion isn't something to 'fix' or "overcome." If you recharge with alone time, enjoy deep oneonone conversations, or prefer a cozy night in over a crowded party, that is not just okay—that is great. Introverts bring incredible qualities to relationships, like empathy, thoughtfulness, and an ability to listen. These are qualities that build lasting, meaningful connections.
- Embrace Your Intellectual Side: For those of us who are drawn to learning, curiosity, and deep dives into topics we love, this intellectual side is a gift. Whether you are a fan of scifi theory, can rattle off random facts about history, or enjoy creating tech solutions in your spare time, these are things that make you, you. People who appreciate these qualities will find them attractive, and they will add richness to your relationships.
- Balance Family Traditions with Personal Needs: embrace the richness of (Indian) family traditions while setting boundaries that honor your introverted nature. Participate meaningfully in cultural rituals without overextending yourself, and work with your partner to create shared traditions that reflect both family values and your individual preferences. Open communication and flexibility are key to harmonizing these influences in your relationships.

SelfReflection Tip: Take a moment to list the qualities, hobbies, and quirks you are proud of. Put this list somewhere you will see it regularly as a reminder of what makes you unique—and valuable.

2. Practice Small Acts of SelfAcceptance Every Day

Selfconfidence does not happen in one big leap. Instead, it is built gradually through small, everyday acts of selfacceptance. These moments reinforce your sense of worth and make it easier to bring your authentic self to any relationship.

- Celebrate Your Small Wins: Confidence grows when you recognize your achievements, no matter how small. Did you share a hobby you usually keep private? That is a win. Did you speak up about a preference on a date? Another win. These small steps toward expressing yourself build up over time and make it easier to be open with future partners.
- Release SelfJudgment: It is easy to fall into the trap of selfcriticism, especially if you have felt pressure to 'fit in' in the past. Try to let go of the urge to judge yourself harshly. Instead, practice selfcompassion. If you are nervous about sharing something personal, remind yourself that being vulnerable is part of what makes connections genuine. There's no one way to 'be' in a relationship, so give yourself permission to be you.
- See Vulnerability as a Strength: Opening up about who you are, including the things that make you feel a little awkward, takes courage. Sharing your interests, from a niche movie genre to a passion project, is a powerful way to invite someone into your world. When you embrace vulnerability, you are showing that you trust someone enough to be real with them—something that, in itself, builds trust and connection.

Daily Confidence Tip: At the end of each day, write down one small way you showed up as your true self.

Reflect on how it felt and use that positive feeling to keep building confidence step by step.

3. Bring Your Authentic Self to Every Interaction

A strong relationship is not about trying to impress someone or hiding parts of yourself. It is about creating a connection where you feel safe to be genuine. The more you can bring your real self to the table, the more you will attract people who appreciate you for exactly who you are.

- Share Your Interests Openly: If you are on a date and your favorite show, hobby, or activity comes up, talk about it with pride. Instead of downplaying it with, "I know it's kind of nerdy, but…" say, "I really enjoy this—let me tell you why!" When you share openly, you give your date a chance to see what lights you up. This confidence is contagious and inviting.
- Express Your Needs Without Apology: Confidence also means being comfortable enough to communicate what you need. If you need alone time to recharge, say it. If a particular setting makes you uncomfortable, let your date know. By expressing your needs honestly, you are setting the tone for a relationship built on respect and understanding.
- Cultivate Curiosity About Your Partner: Just as you bring your unique qualities to the table, so does the other person. Show interest in their story, listen to what they are passionate about, and celebrate their individuality. Relationships thrive on mutual respect and curiosity. When you embrace your uniqueness, you naturally

attract people who are also comfortable being themselves.

Authenticity Tip: Practice sharing small personal details as you get comfortable. You do not need to reveal everything at once—take it at your own pace. Authenticity builds naturally and becomes easier over time.

Looking Ahead with Confidence

As you move forward, remember that finding confidence in yourself is a journey that does not end here. With each new experience, date, or connection, you will learn more about who you are and what you bring to a relationship. Embracing your individuality is what allows you to connect meaningfully with others, and it is what ultimately leads to relationships that feel real and fulfilling.

- Trust That Being Yourself is Enough: The right partner will not expect you to change or fit into a mold. They will appreciate your quirks, respect your boundaries, and enjoy discovering all the layers that make you who you are. When you feel good about who you are, you bring that energy into every relationship, setting the stage for authentic, lasting connections.
- Remember That Confidence is a Practice: Confidence is not a destination—it is something you build a little each day. Some days will feel easier than others, and that is okay. As long as you keep making small choices to embrace your true self, you are building a foundation

for confidence that will carry you through every stage of life.

- Enjoy the Journey: This journey is yours, and every experience adds to the story of your life. Embrace each moment, each lesson, and each new connection. When you look back, you will see how each step brought you closer to becoming the person you want to be—and finding the connection you are truly seeking.

Learning from Your Journey

This whole journey of dating, selfdiscovery, and growth has not been easy—and it is definitely not something that everyone takes on with as much intention as you have. Each step, from the first time you signed up for a dating app to every moment of reflection afterward, has taught you something important about yourself. Now's the time to acknowledge what you have learned, recognize how you have grown, and carry those lessons forward. This is what prepares you for what is next, giving you a solid foundation for future relationships and a deeper understanding of who you are and what matters to you.

In this section, we will look back with appreciation, pull out the insights that have shaped you, and get ready to take them into your future. Each lesson is yours to keep, a reminder of what you have experienced and how it has helped you become the person you are today.

1. Look Back on What You have Learned About Relationships

One of the first things to do when reflecting on your journey is to see how your perspective on relationships has evolved. Maybe you started with a very specific idea of what you wanted, only to realize that what truly matters to you now has shifted. That is a good thing. It means you are growing.

- Clarify What Really Matters in a Partner: Chances are, you have discovered some qualities that you genuinely appreciate and others that just do not work for you. Maybe you have realized that kindness, patience, or shared humor are more important than you originally thought. Or maybe you have learned that it is not enough just to have similar interests—you want someone who respects your boundaries and understands your need for space. By knowing what truly matters, you will recognize the right qualities when they come your way.
- Recognize What Makes a Relationship Feel Good:
- Beyond surface level compatibility, you have probably started to notice what makes you feel truly at ease with someone. This might mean valuing communication styles that feel natural or realizing that shared values make you feel connected. These discoveries are gold. They help you avoid relationships that feel forced and instead guide you toward connections that feel genuine.
- Appreciate How Your Boundaries Have Evolved: Each relationship teaches us more about what we need to feel respected and comfortable. Maybe you have learned to communicate your needs more clearly, or you have found that setting certain boundaries helps you feel secure. Your boundaries are a way of honoring yourself

and recognizing them is a huge part of finding lasting happiness.

Reflection Tip: Jot down a list of what you value most in a partner and in a relationship. These insights are the result of real experiences, and they are the guideposts that will help you make choices that align with who you are.

2. Celebrate the Growth You have Experienced

Dating and relationships can sometimes test us in unexpected ways. It is natural to feel moments of selfdoubt or even frustration along the way. But here is the thing: these challenges have made you stronger. Every experience—whether it led to a lasting connection, or a lesson learned—has contributed to your growth.

- Acknowledge Moments of Courage and Vulnerability: Showing up authentically takes courage, especially when you are putting yourself out there. Think back to those moments when you chose to be honest about who you are, when you shared something personal, or when you stayed true to your values. Every time you did this, you were building confidence in being yourself, and that is worth celebrating.
- Recognize When You Put SelfRespect First: There's a certain kind of growth that comes from choosing selfrespect, even if it means stepping away from a connection. If you ever walked away from a relationship because it did not feel right, or if you set a boundary when it felt necessary, that is a moment to honor. Choosing selfrespect is not always easy, but it is one of

the most powerful acts of selflove you can give yourself.

- Take Pride in Your Resilience: If you have faced setbacks—whether it was rejection, heartbreak, or just a date that did not go well—recognize the resilience it took to keep moving forward. Each time you learned from an experience and continued your journey, you proved to yourself that you can handle whatever comes your way. That resilience will serve you well, no matter what the future holds.

Resilience Tip: Write down a few moments where you made a decision that felt true to you. These are your success stories—proof of the strength you have built through every experience.

3. Carry the Lessons Forward

Each experience, conversation, connection, and even ending has left you with lessons that are yours to keep. These lessons are a toolkit you can use moving forward, giving you clarity on what you want and what you do not and helping you make decisions that support your happiness.

- Understand What Compatibility Means to You:
- You have likely seen by now that compatibility goes beyond shared interests. It is about whether your values align, whether you feel understood, and whether you bring out the best in each other. With this insight, you will be able to focus on connections that feel aligned with your true self.
- Appreciate the Clarity About Your Own Needs:

- Through your experiences, you have probably realized what makes you feel valued and supported. Maybe it is open communication, mutual respect for boundaries, or simply a shared sense of humor. Whatever those needs are, they are valid and important. Honoring them will help you build relationships that are fulfilling.
- Take Pride in Knowing Yourself Better: Dating is not just about finding someone else; it is also about learning who you are. The experiences you have had have shown you your strengths, your preferences, and even the areas where you want to grow. This selfawareness is one of the best gifts you can bring into a relationship.

Lesson Tip: Start a 'lessons learned' list and add to it whenever you realize something new. Over time, this list will show you just how much you have learned, reminding you of your progress and the wisdom you have gained.

In the final section, we'll explore what it means to look toward the future with excitement, set intentions, and embrace the journey ahead with a heart full of possibility.

Paving the Way for the Future

As you finish this book, I want you to know that you have come a long way already. Every experience, insight, and moment of reflection has brought you closer to finding not just a connection but one that feels meaningful and true to you.

This journey is not just about dating; it is about selfdiscovery, growth, and learning to embrace your individuality with confidence. As you look ahead, carry these lessons forward with a sense of possibility. The future is full of new beginnings, and you are ready to meet them with open arms and a clear vision of what matters to you.

In this final section, I will walk you through a few ways to set intentions for your path forward, savor each experience, and keep the door open for all that is to come. Remember, there's no rush. Each step brings you closer to a connection that resonates with who you are. Let's take this moment to look forward with optimism and pride in what you have accomplished.

1. Set Intentions That Reflect Who You Are Today

We all evolve over time, so it is only natural that what you want in a relationship may shift as you grow. Setting intentions for your dating life is less about strict goals and more about understanding the qualities, values, and experiences that matter to you most.

- Think about the Qualities You Want in a Relationship: Maybe you have learned that you value quiet companionship, shared humor, or a mutual respect for personal space. Maybe it is essential for you to have deep conversations or find a partner who enjoys the same geeky pursuits. Whatever it is, let these values guide your choices. Knowing what truly matters to you helps you build relationships that align with your nature and bring you genuine joy.
- Create a Personal Growth Plan, Not Just a Relationship Plan: As someone who thrives on curiosity and learning,

do not lose sight of your personal goals. Relationships are richer when each partner brings a strong sense of self and purpose to the table. Whether it is exploring a new skill, working on your fitness, or getting into a new hobby, growing individually adds to what you bring into a partnership.

- Allow Room for the Unexpected: While it is good to have an idea of what you are looking for, leave some room for surprises. Sometimes, the most meaningful relationships happen when we least expect them. Staying open to possibilities allows you to enjoy the journey without rushing to the finish line.

Intentions Tip: Jot down a few intentions that feel meaningful to you—both in love and in life. Let these intentions be your compass as you move forward.

2. Approach Each New Relationship with Curiosity and Respect

One of the most rewarding things about dating and relationships is the chance to connect with people who have their own unique backgrounds, interests, and quirks. Each relationship you enter, whether it is for a few dates or a few years, brings something valuable to your life.

- Appreciate the Journey, Not Just the Outcome: Not every relationship needs to be 'the one' to be worthwhile. Each connection you make brings its own set of lessons, memories, and experiences. Value these for what they are—steps that enrich your journey, whether or not they lead to a lasting partnership. This mindset frees you to enjoy the moment without the weight of expectations.

- Stay Open to New Perspectives and Shared Experiences: Everyone you meet has something unique to offer, and approaching each date with genuine curiosity opens doors to unexpected connections. You might discover new interests, see things from a different perspective, or even pick up a new favorite hobby. Allowing yourself to explore without judgment creates more fulfilling interactions.
- Treat Each Person as an Individual, Not a Checklist: Each person you meet is more than a list of qualities or shared interests. Respect their individuality as much as you appreciate your own. This not only brings depth to your relationships but also helps you connect on a real, human level where mutual understanding and respect form the foundation.

Curiosity Tip: Make it a habit to ask thoughtful questions and actively listen to the answers. You will find that every date, whether it clicks romantically or not, brings something meaningful to your journey.

A Note to You, the Reader

As you turn the final page of this book, know that I am here to support you beyond these words. If there are specific topics you would like more guidance on or areas where you are seeking deeper insight, please do not hesitate to reach out.

My website, techysoulmates.com, is a place where I will continue sharing tips, resources, and support for fellow introverts, nerds, and geeks who are ready to embrace their journey with confidence. I welcome your questions, feedback, and ideas to make this journey even more meaningful.

Remember, the journey toward love and connection is a marathon, not a sprint. Take your time, enjoy each experience, and let your true self guide you. With every relationship, you are adding to the story of your life—a story that is uniquely yours. Embrace it with joy, knowing that your path forward is filled with possibility.

This is my first book ever written. As an IT entrepreneur, I am one of your fellow introverts. Now I have reached a respectable age, have two beautiful kids and a loving partner, I decided to share my experiences with you. After losing my first date to some friends, learning how to converse, cheat a bit in some small talk, and finally having deep conversations only with the ones dear to me, I have laid everything I know and experienced in this book.

Since I am not a fulltime writer, be gentle with me :) I am still learning and aim to improve this edition. With your feedback, we will make each update even better!

Thank you for allowing me to walk with you through this journey. Here is to the adventures, the learning, and the connections yet to come. The best is ahead.

About The Author

Rohan Patel is an IT and Green Tech entrepreneur, introvert, and proud tech geek who knows the challenges of finding meaningful connections in a fast-paced world firsthand. Born in Latin America, raised in Europe, and rooted in Indian culture, Rohan's multicultural journey has shaped his unique perspective on relationships and self-discovery. In his professional life, he has seen all time zones and worked with many cultures. With his love for sci-fi, Marvel movies, and thoughtful conversations, he is mastered the art of embracing individuality while forging genuine bonds. Rohan shares his experiences in 'How to Find your Techy Soulmate', guiding introverts, nerds, and geeks toward love and connection with authenticity and confidence.